Democracy and the Public Realm

COMPASS PROGRAMME FOR RENEWAL

Democracy and the Public Realm

COMPASS PROGRAMME FOR RENEWAL

Edited by
Hetan Shah
and Sue Goss

in association with
Lawrence & Wishart

London 2007

Lawrence and Wishart Limited
99a Wallis Road
London
E9 5LN
www.lwbooks.co.uk

Compass
Southbank House
Black Prince Road
London SE1 7SJ
www.compassonline.org.uk

First published 2007

Copyright © Compass 2007

British Library Cataloguing in Publication Data.
A catalogue record for this book is available from the British Library

ISBN 978 1905007 516

Members of the Democracy and Public Realm Working Group

Anthony Barnett	Sanjiv Lingayah
Tom Bentley	Guy Lodge
Selina Chen	Vivien Lowndes
Bernard Crick	Su Maddock
Colin Crouch	David Marquand
Peter Facey	Mahua Nandi
Alan Finlayson	Catherine Needham
Nina Fishman	Greg Power
Matthew Flinders	Ben Rogers
Helen Goodman	Mark Ross
Sue Goss (chair)	Jago Russell
Jonathan Harding	Jonathan Rutherford
Paul Hilder	Hetan Shah
Lina Jamoul	Hilary Wainwright
Francesca Klug	David Walker
Neal Lawson	Laurence Whitehead
Daniel Leighton	Robin Wilson
Adam Lent	Richard Wilson
Chris Leslie	Simon Zadek

All contributions were made in a personal capacity. This book aims to reflect the mix of ideas and balance of discussion that emerged, but it should not be taken to be representing the views of any particular member of the working group and individual contributors do not necessarily agree with every conclusion in the book.

About the editors

Hetan Shah is policy director at Compass. He was previously director of the New Economics programme at the new economics foundation, a think tank.

Sue Goss is Principal of National, Regional and Local Services at OPM – the Office of Public Management. She is also deputy editor of the journal *Renewal*.

Acknowledgements

In addition to the members of the working group, we would also like to thank for valuable input and comments: Brendan Martin, Martin Cooper, Martin McIvor, Phil Wyatt, Andrew Judge, David Held, Meg Russell, Des McConaghy, Richard Heller, Lee Roberts, John Earls.

Particular thanks to Sally Davison at Lawrence and Wishart for managing the production and publication of the book.

Thanks to the Joseph Rowntree Reform Trust for providing general funding to Compass. Thanks also to the Barry Amiel and Norman Melburn Trust, Unison, and the following Compass members for providing financial support for the Programme for Renewal: Rebecca Allen, Jack Andrews, Keith Barnard, Victoria Barr, Barbara Barrett, Tony Belton, Clara Bentham, Roy Bentham, Paul Blomfield, Jeffrey Boss, Philip Bradley, John Bull, Joseph Buttle, Margaret Camina, Philip Carter, Peter Cawley, Sarah-Jayne Clifton, Julian Coman, Jeremy Cooper, Paul Cornick, John Crisford, Mike Cuddy, Hugh Davies, Marilyn Evers, Geoff Garrett, Dan Godfrey, Alan Goodfellow, Miranda Grell, John Grieve Smith, Megan Griffith, Ian Hancock, Ryan Heath, David Higgins, Ron Hikel, Del Hosain, Norman Hunt, Alan Hutton, Martin Ignatius Gaughan, George Irvin, Martin John Holst, Philip Jones, Graham Kemp, Peter Kenyon, Maurice Line, Ruth Lister, Margaret Maden, Linda McAvan, Des McConaghy, Peter McGinty, Fiona Millar, Denis Mongon, Andrew Morton, Lawrie Nerva, Neil Nerva, Ray Newton, Wendy Nicholls, Jim Northcott, Richard Pennell, Denis Pethebridge, Anne Rafferty, Howard Reed, Fraser Rennie, Judith Roberts, Tim Roberts, John Robertson, Tony Robinson, Meg Russell, Jonathan Rutherford, Roger Sainsbury, Chris Sewell, Henneke Sharif, Eric Shaw, Victoria Silver, Peter Smith, Nigel Stanley, Jean Stead, Steve Strong, Kathy Sutton, Lindsay Thomas, Alan Tomlinson, Glyn Tudor, Bob Tutton, Giovanni Vitulli, Laurence Whitehead, Larry Whitty, David Williams, Barbara Williams, Robin Woodburn, Richard Young.

Contents

The Compass Programme for Renewal

Compass is a pressure group providing direction to people and organisations who want a more democratic and equal society.

The historic project for social justice and democracy has stalled and is in urgent need of renewal. After the failings of post-war socialism, the rise of Thatcherism in Britain and the domination of neo-liberal values and practices across much of the world, the response of New Labour has been mixed.

New Labour was a creation of pessimistic times. Now, over a dozen years since its birth, its legacy could be described as good in parts. Yes, it has humanised more elements of a rampant market than the Tories ever would have done, but, paradoxically, it has also deepened the grip of the market on society.

Crucially, New Labour adapted itself to the economic rationalism of the neo-liberal project rather than attempt to go beyond this debilitating hegemony. It has failed to break with the old ways of doing politics, and has not responded to the new threats of the market. The problem with New Labour is that it is neither new enough, nor Labour enough. It is a project that has run out of steam.

Building on the partial successes of New Labour, but also learning from its failures, it is time to think again. The Compass Programme for Renewal is the start of that process. Launched just after the 2005 general election, the programme is an ambitious attempt to rethink ideas and strategies for a more equal and democratic society. In the process it offers a space to build alliances between individuals and organisations who share the goals of Compass, so that they may over time become a reality. It is to the synthesis of ideas and organisation that Compass aspires.

The central objective of this politics is to enable people to become the masters of their own destiny. As Gandhi described, we want to be the change we wish to see in the world. Markets have an important but necessarily restricted role to play: the ability to manage our world can only be achieved by working together as citizens, not as individualised consumers.

For freedom to flourish, we need more than greater equality as individuals, so we can all live fulfilled lives. We also need the institutions and processes that will allow us to act together to manage the world around us. True choice requires the possibility that we might change the terms of choices offered to us – to want, and be able to build, a different kind of world.

There are three interlocking elements to this renewal process:

- A vision of a good society – to fuel our political aspirations
- A new political economy that supports this vision – exploring how we can become more enterprising and creative, but also manage markets for the good of society as a whole, at the same time sustaining the life of the planet

- A revival of democracy and the public realm, so that we have the capability to withstand the pressures of an over-encroaching market, and to act collaboratively to determine both what the good society is, and how to progress towards it.

Democracy and the Public Realm is the third in a series of three short books that form the first stage of the Programme for Renewal. They are a collaborative product of many people's time, experience and knowledge. This collaboration includes not just the input of the members of the Working Groups listed in each book, but also submissions from Compass members, findings from desk research, expert interviews, and commissioned 'thinkpieces' that can be seen on the Compass website.

The analysis offered in the books is challenging, and mirrors the threats and opportunities society faces. The policy strategies are not yet systematically formed but are strongly symbolic of a fresh, popular and achievable new politics.

The strategic challenge we face is in linking reforms that are achievable now with a process that transforms our society. The aim is not just a marginally better world, but a different one, where the values of democracy, equality and solidarity, and therefore true freedom, become the new hegemony. Power and principle are two sides of the same coin. How do we balance them effectively?

We don't have all the answers, but these three books mark the start of an overdue debate. We actively welcome contributions and criticisms, in writing or via the space for debate on our website. Compass is also taking the debate out to the countries and regions of Britain with a Renewal Roadshow. Our aim is to engage with progressive organisations and individuals the length and breadth of Britain, including MPs, council leaders, charities, social entrepreneurs, progressive businesses, environmentalists, trade unions, community leaders and think tanks. And after this we aim to conduct a similar process at the European level, in order to build international networks that make a more equal and democratic society a reality.

You can contact Compass as follows:
Website: **www.compassonline.org.uk**
Email: **info@compassonline.org.uk**
Postal address: **Southbank House, London SE1 7SJ**
Telephone: **020 7463 0633**

Foreword

The Compass *Programme for Renewal* trilogy comes to its conclusion where it should – with democracy. There is a strong symmetry between the three elements of the programme. We started with *The Good Society*. What kind of world do we want to create? The central focus was the notion of autonomy – the ability to self-manage our lives by doing it together. The report defined a new malaise – a social recession – caused in the main by the prioritisation of the needs of the market and individuals over society and communities. The second instalment of the programme then examined what kind of *A New Political Economy* would be needed to enable us to manage the market in ways that serve the interests of society, and avoid or minimise the social recession – of inequality, anxiety and unhappiness – from which we are suffering.

And now we conclude with *Democracy and the Public Realm*. Democracy is the missing link for the left. It is the most important belief the left has, and the strongest weapon in our armoury, but it is the one that we turn to the least. When the left define themselves it is usually around concepts of equality and solidarity. Some socialists in the past have even made the mistake of thinking that democracy was dispensable. But for social democrats, democracy is both a means and an end.

The democratic society is the good society. We become autonomous beings because democracy enables and empowers us to do together what we could never achieve alone. It brings us together under rules we understand and support and allows us to build consensus and co-operation through discussion, deliberation and, where necessary, votes. Through democracy we build the organisations, culture and collective confidence to confront and control the destructive consequences of anti-social market forces, while at the same time encouraging their dynamism. Democracy is the best tool we have for bringing markets under control, instead of allowing them to control us.

But democracy is in retreat precisely because New Labour's strategy is based on 'the economy stupid'. Through this emphasis it has moved away from the balance social democracy seeks between, on the one hand, the enterprise, dynamism and innovative powers of the market, and, on the other, the inequality and (now) environmental destruction that free markets unleash. Social democrats have never been anti-capitalist; but, equally, they have always been pro-society.

Markets are not about balance. They are simply a mechanism to maximise profits and turn every democratic space into a commodity to be bought and sold. The goal of competition is the creation of winners and losers. Markets create inequality. In contrast, the basic spirit of democracy is our equality as citizens. So there is a clash. This is why social democracy is about the ideas and institutions that channel and regulate capitalism. If we don't control and harness capitalism we are at its mercy – and mercy is not what it does.

If government no longer tries to control the market in our interests, what is the point of democracy? Why bother voting? One set of market managers is much like the next. No one is stopping the social recession because no one is trying to. Economic blackmail has politicians perpetually on the run. Companies and individuals threaten to decamp to wherever taxes and regulation are lowest. We are in a vicious circle. Politicians feel less and less able to control global market forces, and so they promise less. But as their promises decline, people stop bothering to vote. And the more politicians retreat, the more the market steps in to fill the void. Competition, consumerism and choice have become the new values of British society. The 2007 Unicef report on the comparative well-being of children in rich countries, in which Britain had the worst results, shows just how impoverished these values are.

Why did this happen? One reason is that the institutional form that democracy took in the post-war years – the centralised state – has lost its legitimacy. As the era of mass centralised society came to an end, people no longer accepted being deferential cogs in a machine. Life was becoming more complex, fluid and decentralised. Big, uniform, old-fashioned public services no longer matched the needs of diverse communities. Then, in the 1970s, the right found its voice again. Fuelled and directed by free-market intellects like Hayek and Freedman, the neo-liberal counter-revolutionaries argued that the state was too big, public services largely unnecessary, and freedom would be enhanced if we unleashed capitalism. With the election of Thatcher and then Reagan, taxes were slashed, state utilities sold off, services privatised, unions undermined, the public realm impoverished and local government cut back. The market came to be seen as the answer to all problems.

Twenty years on, the landslide election of New Labour in 1997 signalled the possibility of another swing of the political pendulum. This time 'there was such a thing as society' – the people mattered. As Leader of the Opposition Tony Blair said 'the democratic impulse needs to be strengthened to enable citizens to share decision making that affects them'. But, as we have seen throughout the *Programme for Renewal*, New Labour has offered what is at best a contradictory response to neo-liberalism. The democratic impulse has barely advanced while the market has been given greater and greater prominence. New Labour held out the promise of a new politics – of electoral reform, devolution, trust, and an antidote to Tory sleaze. But the politics were not very new. Reform would be delivered by central targets or the market – not through democratic engagement. The people became either passive recipients of reforms from above or confused consumers of competitive services in health and education.

Even inside the Labour Party, the sweeping changes after 1997 to the way that the party made policy turned out to disempower the members; the National Policy Forum and NEC have been ignored, the party conference agendas have been rigged and activists have been treated to stage-managed conference sessions for the media. Those running the system have no conception of the importance of democracy to maintain and nourish a mass political party. Political mechanisms were modernised, but not political culture.

Giving depth to democracy

What are the young and idealistic to do in this situation? No longer seeing anything to inspire them in New Labour, or any point in formal democracy, they are finding their own ways to change the world. Ellen Pickford from the campaign 'Plane Stupid', who want to control climate change, says: 'The big anti-war march was one of my first political experiences. I saw all those people take to the streets against the war and they were ignored ... This [climate change] is a bigger, more important issue, and I'm not going to allow that to happen again. The only thing left to do is take direct-action'. One of her colleagues explained, 'while we were sitting on that runway, it was amazing to think that, right then, we were stopping carbon emission'.[1] For such activists democracy is about getting involved, being listened to, shaping events; they understand that it is never simply about voting. Clearly, mobilising people on the streets must never replace the formal process of representative politics, but political parties need to be able to connect to social movements that are expressing widespread concerns. Labour is losing a new generation of activists, who feel that they are never listened to.

We think we live in a democracy because we have free elections every four years. But democracy comes in different depths. Ours is shallow and banal. Differences exist between parties but they are being eroded to the extent that too few notice them, and so fewer still bother to vote. Democracy, if it is to work, requires mediating organisations like local government and trade unions, community organisations, public service broadcasters, universities and charities. It demands thought, time, the ability to recognise and honour differences, to deliberate and build consensus. Governments in a hurry, and private companies keen to turn everything into a 'product', have little time to spare for such concerns.

Through the *Programme for Renewal* we have arrived at a definition of modern democracy as being focused around the notion of autonomy and self-management – the ability to control our lives. This is not the same as the consumer freedoms that capitalism offers those of us who can afford them. For even if, as individuals, we can find the money to possess that new car, new dress, or new phone, we can only address the big things in life – what our society is like, how equal we are, the future of the environment – by shaping them together.

This is also true for individual nation states, though there is much more we can do at this level than New Labour will admit – as we outlined in the report *A New Political Economy*. The most urgent problems facing us now can't be solved by nation states acting alone, and social democrats therefore need to think about how we can deliberate and take effective action at global level. This challenge is no more daunting than that faced by progressives in the 1930s, when, after battling against fascism and recession, a new world order was built in the postwar period. Leaders then refused to accept the orthodoxies of the free market, and found new ways to sustain and protect social welfare. Today the issues are environmental, but the principle is the same. We cannot accept the waste and destruction that simply following selfish interests brings. Democracy must go global.

An effective democracy guards us not only against the untrammelled power of the market, but also against the uncontrolled power of the state. The left has always believed that government should be transparent and accountable, and this matters even more now that the government is threatening to constrain civil liberties in the name of the war on terror. During times of danger, it is more, not less important to protect our liberties and rights – they are the things that we value most about the society we have evolved.

Democracy is not just a system of government – it is a vibrant, connected society. 'Our institutions are transformed', says Harvard professor Peter Koestenbaum, 'the moment we decide they are ours to create'.[2] For Compass, the fundamental starting point of the renewal of the centre-left comes with the recognition that both the 'social' and the 'democracy' in social democracy are vital. It is to citizens that real power and responsibility should belong. Government should account to us, and be shaped by us. We believe that, given time, support, resources and opportunities to deliberate, people can be trusted to make 'good' decisions and take more control over their lives.

The top-down, we-know-best approach might have worked in 1945, but it doesn't today. If politicians want effective change, they have to let the people in. If they want to be trusted, they must first show that they trust their citizens. Bernstein, the founding theorist of modern social democracy, said that democracy is 'the weapon in the struggle for socialism, and it is the form in which socialism will be realised'.[3]

Democracy and equality go hand in hand. The greater the depth of our democracy the more equal our nation is likely to be. Political equality prefigures social equality. This is a moral argument, but it is also intensely practical: our argument is that democratic engagement is an effective way of making policy and delivering – better than a system of orders from above, or allowing the market to make all the decisions. Things will work more efficiently and more fairly if democracy is hard-wired into the state, our public realm and more of our companies.

Ultimately our desire for democracy is built on a social conception of what it is to be human. The public realm offers spaces within which each of us is the equal of everyone – where buying and selling gives way to more enduring values. We know that we can be cooperative, caring and compassionate – not just competitive, possessive and individualistic. We realise our potential not simply by acting in isolation, but through collective endeavour, and helping others. There is huge public support for nurturing and protecting these aspects of our lives. Opening up a new 'public realm' through the internet, arts and culture and our shared responsibility for the planet can be popular as well as practical.

We come into this world as equal. Our minds, bodies and the opportunities we have are largely accidents of birth. But we deserve the same chance to be all we can. It is our job as social democrats to ensure we live equal lives of hope and fulfilment. Richard Rumbold, a Leveller and early democratic pioneer, wrote in the language of his day in 1685: 'I am sure there was no man born, marked of God above another, for no man comes into the world with saddle on his back, neither any booted and spurred to ride him'.[4]

There is an inevitable tension between the creative energies of capitalism and the intrinsic worth of those other human experiences – sharing, caring for others, preserving our environment for the future. For the democratic left there is therefore no end point to the journey; there is simply a permanent struggle to try and keep these two in some kind of balance. Part of that struggle is to deepen our democracy, and with it, to create greater equality.

More than ever our lives are out of control. Primarily that is because the needs of the market come before the needs of society. Our response should not be to simply blame the politicians. Instead we must build the ideas and organisations that shape the conditions in which leaders make better decisions. At the same time we can learn from the Levellers, the Chartists, the Suffragettes, trade unionists – and contemporary champions of democracy such as the Citizens Organising Foundation – and make our own world from below. We are the people we have been waiting for.

Neal Lawson
Chair, Compass

Notes

1. Alice O'Keeffe, 'Why the green movement is taking to the streets', *New Statesman*, 6.11.06.

2. In Peter Block and Peter Koestenbaum, *Freedom and Accountability at Work*, Wiley 2003.

3. Quoted in Chris Pierson, *Hard Choices: The Politics of Social Democracy in the 21st Century*, Polity 2001, p24.

4. Quoted in a private paper from David Marquand.

Executive summary

Despite a decade of constitutional reforms under Labour, democracy in the UK is weakening in the light of government centralisation, growing sources of unaccountable power, civil liberties under attack and the privatisation of the public realm. Politicians are among the least trusted groups in society; only 20 per cent of people believe that they can be trusted to tell the truth. A whole stratum of society is excluded from political life – up to a third of unskilled workers and the unemployed do not take part in any political activity including voting. In the last general election young people were half as likely to vote as older people. Few workers feel they have much control over their working lives. We lack effective democratic institutions to deal with the social and environmental challenges we face globally, such as climate change, migration, organised crime and the arms trade.

To deepen democracy we need to create a democratic culture. Reform isn't simply about new laws or government action: we need also to strengthen participatory democracy – democratising civil society, markets, the media and the economy as well as the state. This report concludes that for democracy to flourish, power must move out of the hands of the few, allowing all citizens to shape the world they live in. Some of the proposals we make are longstanding campaign demands for a more democratic society. Some are new.

Our programme for change includes both constitutional measures and proposals to strengthen democracy in civil society:

- Greater power for the UK parliament including powers to initiate legislation
- Abolishing the undefined prerogative powers of the executive
- A fully elected House of Lords
- Devolution of power to local government, and a duty for local authorities to involve local people and communities
- A citizens' debate about PR for national elections, leading to a referendum
- A written constitution
- The abandonment of the misconceived ID cards scheme
- A fundamental culture change in Whitehall to support devolved government, with a radically slimmed down and more strategic centre
- Greater use of deliberative tools at the local level such as citizen's juries, participatory budgeting

- Changes in political parties so that they become campaigning, grass-roots organisations, with caps on donations, and on spending in election campaigns
- Greater disclosure on political lobbying
- The strengthening of civil liberties – educating citizens about the Human Rights Act, and improving access to justice through improved legal aid and courts services
- Protecting and enhancing public service broadcasting – limiting the concentration of media ownership and setting up a Standing Commission on the Media to hold the media to greater public account
- A new partnership approach to innovation in public services – regulating markets to protect public service values; engaging more deeply with users; tailoring services around individual needs; and involving users in rethinking how to achieve social goals
- Protecting the independence of charitable and community organisations
- Support for civil society organisations which enable people to experience democracy; certificated 'national service' for young people volunteering for charities, sports or the arts
- Greater workplace democracy – trades unions taking the lead on ideas about 'good work'; better work-life balance; and emphasis on continuing education
- A commitment to protecting public space – including a moratorium on the sale of school fields and public recreational land to private owners
- New powers for cities to reduce their environmental footprints
- Strengthening the capability of global deliberation to deal with global issues, experimenting with new kinds of international institutions, regulations and networks.

1 The state of democracy and the public realm

WEA Mission Statement

Ubuntu ... is to say, "My humanity is caught up, is inextricably bound up, in what is yours"

Archbishop Desmond Tutu

Democracy, as Thomas Jefferson once said, means government of the people, by the people, for the people. Our rulers too often forget its full meaning. In a true democracy, all persons have an equal voice in their collective government. It is egalitarian by definition. It allows for debate about what the good society looks like. True democracy works in the interests of the commonwealth of the many, not a privileged few. It respects diverse individuals and minorities equally, shaping rules, aspirations, and a society we can all share. Democracy is at the heart of progressive politics. It is about giving voice to the voiceless. Democracy is the route to real liberty – allowing people to lead autonomous lives.

The public realm is the commonwealth: that part of our lives where we are citizens, where it should not matter how much we earn – in the park or library, before the law courts, using the NHS or communicating in the public sphere. The public realm is inhabited by institutions which have traditionally had non-market values, such as academic communities, charities, trade unions and associations. Democracy should build the public realm.

Democracy is a good in and of itself; and it is also 'the best available system for managing power relations among people who disagree about the nature of the common good, among many other things, but who are nonetheless bound to live together'.[1] This means that it is inherently in tension with unaccountable concentrations of power, in the state, market or civil society.

In a capitalist economy rewards are bound to be unequal. Markets cannot address imbalances in power relationships. They simply allow individual choice within the context of widening wealth distribution – however unfair. We should not get rid of markets: they are essential for our economic life, providing dynamism and innovation. But if democracy is to be more than an empty phrase, markets must be better tamed to the service of the good society. The public realm must be secured against the destructive tendencies of market forces.

Politics is the process through which we negotiate collective needs and find ways to achieve goals that we cannot achieve alone. It is a myth to believe that we can lead private lives insulated from the problems of our society – we can only escape temporarily. Government has privileged the idea of individual choice, particularly in public services, as a mechanism to let people take control. But what we want collectively often cannot be achieved through individual choice. It is hard as an individual to choose to have a good public transport system or a safe climate: these are choices that can only be made together. We need a 'better choice of choice' than market individualism offers. Only democracy can provide this.[2]

It is precisely because we need the state to intervene to represent collective needs, and to take action on behalf of all of us against concentrations of private power, that we need, as citizens, to be able to hold the state to account for its actions. An over-powerful and undemocratic state is as dangerous as a weak state.

The state of democracy

New Labour has engaged in a decade of constitutional reforms, including the Human Rights Act, devolution, freedom of information legislation, House of Lords reform, Bank of England independence, the adoption of proportional representation for devolved elections and the creation of a Supreme Court. But paradoxically, after so much legislation, democracy in the UK is still weak and under threat. This is partly because the reforms have been piecemeal, and partly because the government have acted against the grain of their own changes, but also, more broadly, because democracy cannot be inculcated through constitutional change alone.

The UK system has been called an 'elective dictatorship' due to the lack of checks on the power of the government.[3] Judges have become more active in holding government to account since the introduction of the Human Rights Act, but this legislation is misunderstood by the public and maligned by many politicians and the media. The state of the relationship between the executive and judiciary has been described by John Denham, chair of the Home Affairs Select Committee, as amounting to a 'constitutional crisis'. Party politics is seen by most people as irrelevant to their concerns. Politicians are among the least trusted groups in society, with only 20 per cent of people believing that they can be trusted to tell the truth.[4] There seems to be little difference between the parties. The petty 'yah boo' culture of politicking, reflected and amplified by the British media, turns people off. This is reflected in low election turnouts. Politics feels like an insiders' game, self government like a distant dream. The smell of corruption around honours for political donations – to take one example – puts ordinary people off. People's trust in government to solve our problems is low. We feel a general lack of control over our lives and the decisions that affect them.[5]

Government seems very far away from the ordinary citizen, not least because our central government has control of more local services than any other major national government in the world.[6] This makes it hard for the individual citizen to influence decision-making, but, conversely, easier for nationally organised interests and lobbyists, of which business interests are the most powerful. In an era of 'glocalism', where we face global problems that need solutions at the local level – from waste management to transport – this nation-state centralism gets in the way of both the local and the global. This is combined with the fact that we have one of the most secretive governments in the West, as shown by the Hutton and Butler inquiries. Whilst the Freedom of Information Act has opened government up to some extent, there are 36 exemptions to the Act, which are commonly used to withhold information, particularly around current policy decisions.

We have seen the erosion of liberty on a range of fronts over the last few years. There has been the curtailment of rights of protest through laws intended to deal with anti-social behaviour or terrorism, and a new law preventing people from engaging in protest within 1 kilometre of Westminster without authorisation. We have also seen detention without trial for terror suspects, increased police powers, and the looming introduction of ID cards – at a cost of anything from £5 billion (as estimated by the government) to £18 billion (as estimated by *The Financial Times*). The UK has become a surveillance society, with one CCTV camera for every 14 people, and has been rated the worst Western democracy at protecting individual privacy.[7] There is growing evidence that UK airports and airspace has been used by CIA planes in the practice of 'extraordinary rendition' where suspects are flown to states that practice torture with the aim of gaining intelligence. The admirable introduction of the Human Rights Act has provided redress for some of these incursions into our liberties, but the Act has itself been under attack.

Democracy is not just about the nation state: much unaccountable power lies outside of the state, including the media, finance capital and multinational corporations. These are some of the sites of power in today's society, but it is difficult to know how to go about holding them to account. On a smaller scale, few workers feel they have control over their workplace, with only two in five saying that they have a strong influence over their working hours or the organisation of their work.[8] And panning out to a larger scale, we live in an increasingly international and global world, but we lack the governance mechanisms to influence these arenas. The European Union feels remote and it seems impossible to know how to hold international bodies such as the World

Trade Organisation or the International Monetary Fund to account. We lack effective democratic institutions to deal with the social and environmental challenges we face globally, such as climate change, migration, organised crime and the arms trade.

Whilst there is still a great deal of active citizenship and interaction outside of formal politics, such as through the voluntary sector, many people do not have the basic resources to participate in society. Over 11 million people live in poverty, and we have the longest working hours in Europe, making it that much harder to sustain participation. A whole stratum of society is excluded – up to a third of people in socio-economic groups D and E (unskilled workers and the unemployed) do not take part in any political activity including voting. In the last general election young people were half as likely to vote as older people;[9] and around 70 per cent of managerial and professional classes voted whilst only 54 per cent of the unskilled and unemployed did. Therefore it is crucial that any democratic programme does not further entrench the disproportionate influence that the more affluent exercise over politics. Democratic engagement is a function of the access of communities and citizens to assets – from skills to savings. As argued in the other *Programme for Renewal* books, we need a comprehensive redistribution of these.

We live in an increasingly diverse and cosmopolitan society – racially, religiously, sexually and in many other ways. Society is richer for it, from the food we eat to the places we visit on holiday. Diversity does, however, pose challenges for society, and democracy needs to adapt. In a diverse society the bases for citizenship can become more difficult to build. There is less diversity in public life – only 20 per cent of MPs are women and very few ethnic minorities are represented. It can be more difficult to maintain solidarity in a less homogenous society and policy requires more thought and care to prevent a sense of unfairness. There is evidence that in the midst of our diverse society we are becoming more segregated – by class, race and religion.[10] Levels of trust are falling: in the 1950s, 56 per cent of people agreed that most people could be trusted, whereas today only a third of the population agree.

In the face of these tendencies towards division, there is a need for new forms of association. In this context we should welcome the new 'public' virtual spaces, including social networking sites such as MySpace and Bebo, which are linking up many people online. There is also a long standing tradition of networks of association for mutual benefit helping to support the wider public good (as well as of more negative cases). People using social networks often have a strong ethic of mutual respect and the public good, and networks like MySpace may act as a cradle for more solidaristic behaviour in the future. We need new mechanisms which allow people to act together to solve the problems that we collectively face. Issues such as obesity or climate change can only be changed by the co-ordinated actions of the many.[11]

Increasing numbers of people are losing faith in the effectiveness of the political system, and losing trust in both the competence and the integrity of politicians. Instead, people are turning to single-issue politics. And while many single-issue campaigns are important and welcome, this more consumerist approach to politics makes it harder to resolve conflicts of interest between different groups in society – and harder to achieve the 'negotiated compromises' which have been traditionally created through party programmes. If we simply demand solutions to single issues, and if government simply sees governance as about 'delivery', then we reduce ourselves from citizens to consumers.

The failure of politicians to win public trust weakens the capability of our democracy to mediate the range of conflicting interests that exist. Democracies work through the creation of broad alliances of interest and identity – alliances which in the modern world can shift and reform. Politicians should play a crucial role, both by 'representing' different interests and by putting forward competing solutions. Programmes and manifestos help us as citizens to hold political parties to account. The actions of presidents and dictators, without the constraint of parties, are harder to predict and harder to control. But politicians need to renew the process of dialogue with the communities they represent. In the absence of real links back to their electorates, politicians, once they are elected, look upwards for reward and patronage and often seem powerless to their voters.

The changing public realm

Alongside all of this, we are seeing commercial values creeping into public services and the wider public realm. The public realm is shrinking as the market extends into new areas and crowds out values of fairness and collectivism with more commercial and individualistic values. In particular we are seeing commercial values and markets being introduced into the realm of public services on the basis of ideology rather than evidence. This is detrimental to the society we live in, and once we lose the public realm it is not easy to restore.

The values which govern public services and the public realm, and the outcomes which we seek there, must be determined in public – by government and society at large. They should not be corrupted by the internal dynamics of the market. The private sector has a place in the public realm only as a servant, and it is possible for the public to set the rules to ensure that happens.

As argued in *The Good Society*, we need a better account of citizenship. People were in the past treated as subjects and are increasingly being treated as consumers ('customers' of public services). But we are not purely economic men and women – we are also citizens. In his classic work *The Gift Relationship*,

Richard Titmuss highlighted the difference between England and Wales, where blood donors were unpaid, and the US, where they were paid.[12] Titmuss compared the statistics and showed that more people gave blood voluntarily, compared with donations stimulated by financial incentives. He concludes that 'commercialisation of blood and donor relationships represses the expression of altruism', and that, in terms of economic efficiency, it is highly wasteful of blood. This is suggestive of the broader point that a well functioning society treats people not just as consumers but also as citizens, and recognizes that they have responsibilities as well as rights. As citizens they need to be given equal standing, and effective ownership of our political institutions. They have rights: to be included, to have access to basic resources for human flourishing and to meaningful participation. They also have responsibilities – to respect others, recognise their mutual dependence and behave in a way that does not destroy the common good.

Ways forward

Democracy faces multiple challenges. Representative democracy is faltering and needs renewal. Unaccountable power is concentrated in particular sites across society. The market is increasingly unconstrained. Our society faces challenges where we need to act collaboratively more than ever. We need to deepen democracy through more deliberative and participative democratic mechanisms which spread democracy into the 'everyday' of our lives. And we need to foster a stronger public realm and associative democracy, with organisations that bring people together collectively to live and learn together.

The opportunities are there for the taking. People are not apathetic – quite the opposite. But we have been turned off traditional modes of politics, and new structures, fit for the twenty-first century, have not yet been implemented. We want more control over our lives. We want our individual decisions to be beneficial for society. Even as we stand in the queue to check in to a cheap flight we know that it should be more heavily taxed for the sake of our environment. There is a need for innovation by government, civil society and markets to help us act together to create a better world. This implies a new kind of state – working in partnership with people and enabling them to achieve what they want – and it implies a need for more managed markets.

Across the world we are seeing experiments to deepen democracy; these range from changes to national constitutions to smaller scale projects, for example those which allow people to influence their local area.[13] Alongside the rise of representative democracy after 1989, we have seen many different trends to strengthen democratic involvement. Power has been decentralised in many places, including France, India, China, Bolivia and Chile. There has been increased use of referendums, participatory budgeting, citizens' forums, deliberative polling and other methods that give people a greater chance to democratically engage. There is a wealth of new thinking about how the state can play a more intelligent role in producing good outcomes for all through empowering citizens and democratising public service delivery.[14] And civil society is creating all kinds of interventions which allow us to act together to solve problems we cannot tackle alone. For example Pledgebank.com allows people to say they will do something if other people will also pledge to do the same; Global Action Plan is a charity that helps people to change their environmental behaviour in partnership with a group of neighbours, thus building motivation and enjoyment. We need to cultivate more democratic innovations which decentralise power and give people the ability to shape their lives.

We need, then, a democratic politics in the twenty-first century that is pluralist – that responds to the diversity of needs and lifestyles, and engages with people in the ways that suit them. At the same time, given the growing inequality in our society, politics must be egalitarian, ensuring that respect for difference does not reinforce inequalities of power.

The relationship between the state and civil society will always be one of tension – democratic politics is the conversation that keeps the relationship live and empowering rather than oppressive and constraining. The state must be powerful enough to act on our behalf to constrain powerful vested interests, since it is a fantasy to believe that through voluntary means we can substitute for government action. Local and central government need enough leverage to make very rich individuals and companies listen to and comply with the needs of the wider community. But the strength of government comes only with the engagement and consent of civil society. A more solidaristic civil society would make it easier for us to pay attention to each other's need, to compete less and collaborate more. In the era of mass education and direct communication, government is a partnership between government and people. Democracy is not only about voting – it is also a political process, and requires an active engagement in the social activities that underpin the trust and confidence in democracies. There are new democratic experiments at work, especially in civil society, that offer ways to deepen democracy beyond representative government. We need a politics that can make that process healthy, vibrant, fascinating and serious.

Many of the issues that need to be tackled to create a thriving democracy have been discussed in the other *Programme for Renewal* books and therefore this volume should be read alongside those. We need social justice to make sure that all groups have the ability to participate, and each of the previous books put forward agendas for the redistribution of resources and a basic minimum level of economic, human and social capital for all. Both books also addressed the issue of time, which is a necessity for democratic participation, and the importance of care. *The Good Society* also explored ideas for living in a diverse society and creating a new conception of citizenship, while *A New Political Economy* was based on the idea of creating a democratic economy which works for people and planet rather than the other way around. Both books put forward ideas to deal with major issues that we face, in particular environmental sustainability.

This book will not go over the ground covered by the other two volumes but will consider what else needs to be done to create a vibrant democracy and a strong public realm. *Democracy and the Public Realm* puts forward both shorter and longer term ideas about how we could move towards a better democracy. But more important than any particular policy proposal is the direction of travel and the principles that underlie this approach. There is no merit in producing a static blueprint: policy needs to be responsive and keep evolving. Democracy is a process not an end state.

2 A new political culture of democracy

Too often the debate about democracy has been focused on the creation of constitutional structures. Whilst these are necessary, they are not sufficient. To create a thriving democracy we need to challenge the culture of consumerism, the adversarialism of politics, the nature of political campaigning, the role of the media, cynicism about political values and the decline of political parties.[15] Time is also a key issue: as we work longer hours we have less time to act as citizens.[16]

There are a number of key areas where we can strengthen democratic culture. We can create better opportunities for participative politics, especially for the worst off. We need desperately to change the way that party politics operates and we need a new culture of freedom of information. These steps would help create a culture that understands democracy as a fundamental step to leading our lives freely and autonomously.

Participative politics

We should spread democratic opportunity through all levels of the political system. There are many examples of different kinds of deliberative and participative mechanisms which could be used, from citizens' juries to participatory budgeting.[17] Government, especially central government, badly needs opening up. And participation can nurture an ethos of citizenship – of collective decision-making and a sense of responsibility. Research shows that participative decisions have more 'buy-in' and better levels of compliance.

Participation must, however, be engaged in carefully: badly executed participation is often worse than no participation at all.[18] As citizens we want opportunities to participate when we want to, but also the opportunity not to when we do not want to. Most people will only want to participate on specific issues at specific times – often when something is going wrong. If people are invited to get involved (e.g. in shaping a public service or feeding into policy-making), it should be clear to all what power they have to influence. There has been too little participation that is backed up with real power.

Participatory opportunities must be focused on giving voice to those who do not have it. Much participative activity only opens up processes to those who are already powerful. The report of the Commission on Poverty, Participation and

Power showed that people in poverty are usually not included in decision-making processes, even those directly affecting them.[19] Research by the Electoral Commission and the Hansard Society shows that only 32 per cent of manual workers and non working people say they would contact their MP, compared to 63 per cent of professional and non-manual workers. People living in poverty should be involved in the design, implementation and evaluation of policy. This includes policy on poverty, but should be much wider, to include all kinds of policy-making. For example, the planning system could use innovations such as 'Planning for Real', which involves the public in planning decisions creatively through building a 3D model of the community.[20] Government should review where the benefits system prevents people from getting involved. There needs to be adequate funding for increased participation in decision-making by excluded people, including benefit recipients, carers and people with disabilities, and government staff need training and capacity-building so that they can construct good processes.

It is not enough to change the structures and open government up. We learn to be citizens through doing – we need to give people, especially the most marginalised, ways into citizenship and the resources they need to participate when they want to. The institutions which have in the past given people access to political ideas and activity, such as trade unions, churches and political parties, are in decline. Therefore we need to expand people's political knowledge and understanding and give them opportunities to understand better how the political world works. Citizenship education has been a good start, but it is not taken very seriously. It should be established as a full part of the curriculum rather than taught through other subjects. MPs should also be able to communicate more with their constituents, and Parliament should be better at communicating with citizens about the work that is done in Westminster.[21] The public want a conversation not just consultation.[22] Therefore democratisation is not just about re-engaging citizens with existing linear processes of representation, but is a question of creating more open and collaborative relationships in politics, of the sort we have elsewhere in life.

Changing representative politics

We cannot restore trust and legitimacy through institutional change. To be trusted, politicians must be trustworthy. We need to challenge the way that politicians are perceived and behave. Values of civility, reciprocity and mutuality cannot be upheld by making speeches and setting rules: they require an example to be set through the behaviour of political and community leaders. To nourish and support deliberation and dialogue as forms of governance would require a change in the way that politicians behave – ceasing to 'tell' and 'spin' and learning to listen, disclose and have meaningful conversations. The Fabian Society has put forward the idea of a ten point political charter, which all politicians are encouraged to sign up to.[23] The charter is as follows:

- Frankness about the purpose of politics: Admitting that politics is hard, that tough choices have to be made, and that not everyone can win all the time. Celebrating the centrality of debate, negotiation and compromise.

- Carving out a distinct political sphere: Making clear that parties and politicians are not products in a market, that politics is governed by different rules, and that citizenship can fulfil human aspirations that consumerism cannot.

- Offering political leadership: Acknowledging that, whilst politicians must of course be responsive to voters, it is also their role to spell out the big choices facing society.

- Making values explicit: Explaining the vision that underlies policy and how this underpins particular decisions. Resisting the 'catch-all' party by admitting that action is guided by values, and spelling out what these values are.

- Honesty about constraints, including the financial constraints within which policy decisions are taken, and the responsibilities of others, including citizens, to play a part in bringing about change.

- Being prepared to show fallibility: Admitting mistakes, explaining changes of policy and stating when an answer is unknown or impossible to give.

- Rejecting opposition for opposition's sake: Being prepared to state when politicians from other parties are right. Not attacking opponents unless an alternative course of action is clear and achievable, and not getting trapped by journalists into knee jerk opposition.

- Responsible campaigning: Avoiding both exaggerated promises and corrosive attacks on the opposition.

- Defending political parties: Not forgetting how all current politicians arrived in office, and being explicit about how parties' continued health is essential to the system.

- Not exploiting lack of voter trust: Perhaps most important of all, not seeking short term gain from the current culture of disengagement. Respecting the integrity of opponents and resisting allegations of dishonesty or corruption except in the rare and isolated circumstances where these are justified. Instead promoting politicians – including those of opposing parties – as hardworking individuals driven by a sense of duty and belief in building a better society.

Building support for a charter like this would immensely help the role that politicians play in society, which in turn would help to change the culture of politics that exists at the moment.

But we, the public, have to grow up too. Public expectations are a real issue – we, the public, demand more and more, and political parties are encouraged to promise that they can deliver these desires. We need to create a mature environment in which a discussion can take place about the limits of the state and the appropriate balance between individual rights and responsibilities. Politicians should make public expectations more realistic rather than enflaming them.

Political parties

Political parties are important to politics. Representative democracy is based on maximising the common good through balancing competing interests, and political parties play a crucial role in this.[24] At their best they help create a debate about different ideas of the good society. But political parties need to renew themselves structurally and culturally, as they are in serious decline.[25] Parties as we know them came about in the nineteenth century, and their structures and processes are not fit for the modern age.

Parties should remake themselves as civic institutions.[26] They could be given a 'public benefit status' for work done that is similar to that of charities, such as research and civic action, with tax relief for donations and funding related to membership levels. Becoming more grass roots requires parties to spend less on marketing. To help this there should be caps on both donations and spending during election campaigns. This would limit the influence of wealthy donors and prevent parties being focused purely on mass advertising, which is of little benefit to democracy.

At present the bigger parties are hollowed-out shells. They are highly centralised and do not offer members very much power, particularly over policy. But, just as in other areas explored in this book, command and control will not work. Parties need to become more open to debate, allowing members to play a far more active role in policy formulation between elections. One good example here is George Papandreou in Greece, who has renewed his party through an open conversation involving 150,000 people feeding in their political ideas. All of this implies the need for more democratic structures. They need to be more representative of the society we live in today, in membership and culture, and act as a better bridge between local and national politics. This could come from a greater focus on the local – from improving constituency offices to more local party conferences. The challenge for parties is to both listen and lead, and to help create new social alliances capable of facing the challenges of the future.

Freedom of information

Freedom of information is a crucial component in creating a democratic political culture. The Freedom of Information Act has led to some opening up in Britain's politics, with journalists in particular using the Act to good effect, including their uncovering of university investments in arms companies and the food industry's lobbying of the Food Standards Authority to minimise publicity when withdrawing unsafe products. But the legislation was watered down before it was made law, and in practice much information is still withheld, particularly on issues of legal or policy advice, and the background to current government decisions.

We need stronger freedom of information, similar to the system in the United States. In particular private company deals which affect the public realm (for example in the arenas of Private Finance Initiatives or Public Private Partnerships) need to be much more transparent. At present the contracts for such deals (such as the cost of ID cards) are secret, because of 'commercial sensitivity'. We should also promote environmental democracy – the idea that we should all have access to environmental information, since we are all affected by the outcome. People need the basic facts to become active citizens in resolving issues that affect them. This has been recognised to some extent by the Environment Information Regulations 2004, which provide stronger rights of access than the Freedom of Information Act.

Symbols of democracy

Another part of the solution is to update the symbols of democracy. Our symbols of democratic culture are weak: the political culture remains saturated with pre-democratic norms and symbols – the monarchy itself, the House of Lords, the honours list – and, much more importantly, crucial pre-democratic institutions and doctrines have survived effectively unchanged into the democratic era. One major example is the Royal Prerogative, which allows the government to act without parliamentary approval on a variety of matters, including going to war. Another is the doctrine that civil servants are servants of the Crown – which in practice means the government – and not of the public or of Parliament. Yet another is the absence (in England) of any formal constitutional provisions protecting lower tiers of government from interference with (or even abolition by) the central executive. (Scotland and Wales are now in a different position thanks to the devolution statutes.) We need reform to address these democratic deficiencies; and we need to create new symbols of democracy for Britain, including celebrating the more democratic aspects of our heritage, such as the Leveller and Chartist movements.

By changing the nature of party politics, the secretive culture of government and the symbols of democracy, and by opening government up through better participative processes, we could move towards a far stronger democratic culture.

What else can be done to create a more democratic culture? *The Good Society* and *A New Political Economy* put forward ideas about time, consumption, citizenship and other issues which would help create cultural change. And some of the other chapters in this volume consider a number of issues which will contribute to this: embedding human rights; re-evaluating the role of the media in democracy; strengthening civil society; and engaging in public service reform, so that the public sector no longer apes the private sector but is a protected part of the public realm. But a key starting point would be to devolve power, which is the focus of the next chapter.

3 Devolution

The UK has one of the most centralised governments in the world, in terms both of the raising of finance and the management of local services; and England is especially centralised.[27] Under New Labour constitutional reform has reduced the power of Westminster to some extent, but this has been primarily by transferring power to other politicians, judges and professionals, rather than to the people. All of this is a major cause of disengagement from formal politics – government seems distant, unresponsive and closed. The 2007 Local Government White Paper is a welcome shift in the other direction, but does not go nearly far enough in decentralising power to local government and local communities.

Decentralisation has been a worldwide trend – from India and China to Sweden and France. Trust tends to be much higher in local institutions than in national ones. While not all politics is local and people inhabit many communities of interest which are not local, geography is still important to us and the way our local communities are run should be more democratic. However, the UK is the most centralised country in Europe. Local politics has been hollowed out by a lack of power, autonomy and accountability. But our neighbourhoods, towns, cities and communities are vital everyday arenas in which isolated individuals come up against the forces of globalisation; they are places in which conflicts of interest could be negotiated at the local level, so that habits of participatory democracy could grow, and faith in collective action and decision-making be rekindled. And it is only really at the local level that government can successfully be 'joined up'.

We need a new constitutional settlement between central and local government, and there are two main principles to how we should devolve power. First, devolved power must be transferred not to unaccountable or self-selecting elites, but to vibrant local democracies in which representation, participation and accountability are harnessed to each other. This will require strengthening people's capacity to participate, as discussed in the chapters on the culture of democracy and on civil society. Secondly, in parallel with these arrangements for local variety and responsiveness, frameworks for redistribution between localities must be strengthened. Managing the relationship between equality and diversity is one of the great challenges for any devolutionary agenda. Basic equality is the starting point to allow people to lead free and democratic lives. At the national level there is a crucial role for the state to deal with inequality, but, beyond this, the only way to manage this dynamic tension between equality and diversity is through democratic processes. (It is of course a myth that centralism produces equal outcomes – for example, in 1980 the Black Report showed the major inequalities that existed in a nationally directed health system.) The shape of the good life locally may differ from place to place, from rural village to inner-city area; but the devolution of power requires redistribution within a stronger overall framework of solidarity.

A devolved governance structure

We need a new relationship between tiers of government, one which is more focused on strategy and co-ordination and less on micromanagement from the centre. A devolution framework would create a 'hub and spoke' model, placing the locality at the heart of the structure, with a small enabling infrastructure at regional level and Whitehall at the periphery. The different parts of government would work to support one another, like a wheel. Localities could negotiate with the centre about the way they intended to achieve nationally prescribed goals and standards, and would try to win support and resources for local priorities.

The community leadership role expected of a democratically elected council should be a strong, rather than a weak one. Local government, in partnership through Local Strategic Partnerships, should have the leverage to make things happen on behalf of local citizens. They should lead consultation about local outcomes, and allocate resources and create the organisational architecture to deliver those outcomes. They should provide some services themselves; but also manage markets to secure public good in services provided by others. They are guardians of the local public realm. Most importantly, they should create the conditions for effective governance, ensuring citizens have equal access to services and are equally able to hold providers and commissioners to account.

At the regional level, what would be needed is a fluid network of powerful enablers, accountable either to a regional electorate or to the centre. They would be small, tight and strategic in focus, not distracted by detailed process control. They would operate across government 'silos', promote enterprise and innovation and be capable of funding and sponsoring major experimental projects (for example long term transport projects). They would also support innovation and share expertise, create a strong evidence base around the regional economy and manage larger regional markets.

This would leave a far smaller civil service at the centre, and here there could be even more radical reform. Instead of vast central departments, what is needed are highly skilled strategic thinkers; and a small number of experienced policy specialists, many of whom might be seconded from outside. Liberated from the fiction of delivery, civil servants could concentrate on what they do best: creating the framework of legislation, policy, finance and sanctions to secure government goals in a way that accords with a fluid, innovative and pluralist network of providers. The work process of the civil service could shift to highly focused, multi-disciplinary policy teams, organised around each of the government's key policy goals instead of in departmental silos.

Alongside these would be knowledge management and innovation teams, responsible for research and development and bringing together thinkers and experts from the field to test out radical ideas. These could be supported by a serious long-term research capability, based in universities, and protected from short-term ministerial preoccupations. Reforming ministerial responsibility, as suggested in the next chapter, would also improve the performance of civil servants and enable them to be held to greater account. Ministers can devolve power, but until they can also devolve accountability and blame, little will change. At present, if a university closes its chemistry department it is the Secretary of State for Education who gets grilled on the *Today* programme.

With smaller cross-boundary policy teams, duplication would reduce and collective memory and experience would build. Government advice could increasingly come directly from academics, practitioners, community leaders and professionals. Instead of cumbersome guidance, a network of conversations between the centre, regions and localities would transmit learning about what was happening on the ground. The role of the centre would be to check for value for money, and there would still have to be consequences for poor performance. And a process such as Comprehensive Performance Assessment should continue, but should be more transparent; shared access to data could lead to collaborative discussions of problems in delivery, and challenge and dialogue could replace rigid process control. Inspection services should be seen as clearly independent of government and accountable to the public – able to comment fearlessly on and investigate the effectiveness of all levels of government in the public interest.

This is not a call for more 'restructuring' of civil service departments, but for a fundamental change in work practice and culture. This will be easier if the civil service is opened up, with far more movement between government, local government and other public service posts; this will help to break the 'bureaucratic mindset' in which the centre is always superior in the hierarchy: there should be as much prestige in running a great city as in running a government department. Government would need to think about long-term workforce planning across public services, offering retraining to young civil servants to move across into the more exciting localities where delivery really happens. The era of targets could be succeeded by constant, real-time performance improvement, driven at the front line instead of at the centre. There would be open access to performance data for the public as well as government. There could also be regular challenge dialogues between agencies and their stakeholders, exploring how well public money is being spent, and how successfully outcomes are being achieved.

Strengthening the local

Significant powers should be shifted to local democratic control by the end of the next Parliament. At present there is a vicious circle: central government will not devolve power until local government proves itself to be more competent, but local government cannot do this until there is greater devolution. There are a number of practical ways in which devolution could be taken forward in line with the overall vision above. Local democracy could be given greater power across the local public services to direct, coordinate and set strategic priorities, in particular for community policing and aspects of public health. Responsibilities for local transport, jobs, environmental sustainability and learning could be transferred to local and regional government from Whitehall and the quangos. Beyond a core of national entitlements, central targets and inspections should be replaced by local accountability and public priorities wherever possible. The majority of top-down constraints on how local funds are spent and raised could be lifted, and the tax base shifted progressively from national to local level. This rebalancing would need to be accompanied by a strengthening of financial equalisation between rich and poor areas.

We also need to open up local governance through a more participatory, 'everyday' democracy. Public authorities and local government in particular should be given a duty of public involvement: to engage citizens in helping to set their visions, priorities, targets or budgets, and empower them with the information to do so. Local authorities could be encouraged to innovate in this area, by national government making freedoms and flexibilities available more rapidly to those prepared to devolve real collective power and influence to citizens. Frameworks of neighbourhood governance below strategic local government could be empowered on everyday issues of safety and liveability, with powers to act directly, raise funds, influence public authorities and call them to account through means such as democratic neighbourhood councils and participatory planning. The proposals in the 2007 local government White Paper can be built upon to make participative democracy a reality – but only if government at local and regional level has real power.

We can learn from examples across the world, such as the People's Planning Campaign from Kerala in India. Around 2 million people attended local meetings to generate proposals which were fed into village plans, which in turn were integrated at the regional level. Citizens were given training in planning issues and supported by experts such as engineers to help understand technical issues where necessary. The process shows how local decision-making can feed into higher level plans.[28]

There are many innovations in local democracy which can be built upon.[29] Citizens' juries, open space events, deliberative polling, planning for real exercises and so on have proven their worth. Participatory budgeting in Porto Alegre in Brazil, introduced in response to the corruption of local government expenditure, was a major and exciting innovation. The aim there was to transform the budget into an accountable and bottom-up system based on the city dwellers' needs. It has had phenomenal success, with around 100,000 people (from around 1.3 million inhabitants) participating in the opening up of the budgetary process. During the first seven years of participatory budgeting the share of households with access to water services increased from 80 per cent to 98 per cent and the share with access to sanitation increased from 46 per cent to 85 per cent.

One of the most important aspects of these democratic mechanisms is the deliberative aspect, where citizens take the time to consider, think and change their minds. This is central to collective decision-making, which requires the balancing of competing interests rather than a purely single-issue focus to the exclusion of other considerations. Hence we need to find and promote those democratic mechanisms that promote this kind of holistic thinking. Deliberative mechanisms lead to a radically different kind of democracy from the aggressive 'pale, male and stale' grandstanding that people associate with Westminster. While we should not get carried away – as citizens our time is limited and we will always want our democratic representatives to take many decisions on our behalf – direct and deliberative democracy provides an essential complement to representative democracy, enabling citizens to help steer complex decisions and ensuring government hears many different voices. The strengthening of local democratic decision-making and participation would open up a richer and more meaningful field for local politics, driving up turnout and enlivening competition, to the benefit of citizens and politics alike.

Cities and regions need to take more account of their environmental footprints and to have the requisite powers to deal with these. We need to look around for inspiration as to what can be done. For example, China is building Dongtan, an ecocity, for 2010, based on the principle of being self-sustaining in energy, water and food, with no greenhouse gas emissions from transport. But we don't need to look so far away for good models – the Nottingham Agreement has many UK signatories, and the London Sustainable Development Framework is also an exemplar. Our cities and regions need the power to aim for real sustainability.

It is at local level that government can cope with complexity. The social outcomes that public agencies want to achieve are influenced by many interacting causes, which impact differently on each place; and it is only there – be it a large city, a county, a network of villages, a neighbourhood – that people can work together to understand the impact of current actions and plan solutions that work. By devolving power we could move towards a far more effective and democratic governance.

4 UK constitutional reform

The government has engaged in a wide programme of constitutional reforms. But although some individual measures have been important steps forward, they have been made piecemeal, and lack coherence. Power has, if anything, become more concentrated in Whitehall, and within Whitehall in the hands of the Prime Minister and his appointees. The Butler report shows the extent to which the government is run by a small number of people in Downing Street – and not even by the Cabinet.

We need a constitutional settlement with better checks and balances. An over-powerful executive is more liable to make bad mistakes – from the invasion of Iraq to the introduction of ID cards. While the judiciary is still able to challenge the executive under EU and human rights legislation, parliament is weak and we need to strengthen its powers.

The constitution matters not just as a set of rules: it also embodies and transmits values. Since we have no written constitution we have no public statement of what the democratic values we hold actually are, and why they are important. Of course our unwritten constitution does reflect values – often pre-democratic values, or those that reflect a notion of democratic majoritarianism, a society where the winner takes all. We need a new explicit constitutional settlement, that entrenches the sovereignty of the people, but creates also a new democratic order that can match the problems of the twenty-first century – one that is pluralist, deliberative and, where possible, consensual. A written constitution would form the framework for such a settlement, but we also need to develop a political culture that can make such a constitution come alive.

The role of parliament

The British public's faith in its parliament is amongst the lowest in Europe. A recent Eurobarometer poll would have put the UK at the bottom were it not for the even more sceptical electorates of the former-Soviet bloc countries. Parliament – both Commons and Lords – needs to recapture public support. It is only likely to do this if it becomes more effective in carrying out its core tasks: holding government to account, scrutinising legislation and representing the public interest.

The executive's undefined prerogative powers should be abolished. It should not be possible for ministers to make critical decisions, such as on peace or war, without an express resolution (rather than a consultative vote) of the House of Commons. Nor should the monarch appoint ministers: her role should be replaced by an affirmative post-election resolution of the house for a government to be formed. A constructive vote of no confidence, as in Germany, could be required for government to be brought down.

Parliament needs a more deliberative style. The party political battle at Westminster has served a purpose by illuminating key aspects of contentious issues. But the decline of ideology means that the adversarialism in the chamber is increasingly manufactured – a state that is obvious to everyone but the MPs who participate in it.

We need to find ways of allowing MPs to escape the party political straitjacket from time to time. This is not an argument for doing away with party politics, but an acceptance that, increasingly, issues in parliament do not divide along neat left-right lines. It would make more sense for party whips to apply three-line whips more sparingly, thus avoiding the rising number of often unnecessary rebellions. Giving MPs greater latitude on issues that are not critical to the government's (or opposition's) platforms would perhaps make MPs look more like rational political actors to the public. It would also emphasise the issues where there was genuine ideological difference, and highlight more effectively what was at stake.

It is outside the chamber that more significant changes can be made, however. The select committees enable MPs to work as cross-party teams away from the party political pantomime of the chamber, and offer a far more thorough form of scrutiny than anywhere else in parliament. Every backbench MP should be on a select committee. Of the 400-plus backbenchers at Westminster, only 250 or so currently have a role on the select committees. Select committees should be responsible for scrutinising and taking public evidence on legislation, replacing the standing committees whose members are subject to the party whip in a way that select committees are not. The committees need a dedicated period when the chamber is not sitting, perhaps one day a week, or one whole week each month.

Taking committee work seriously – in ways that are common in most other parliaments – would increase the expertise and independence of our politicians. It would also increase the capacity of parliament. The committees need to be given more power and more capacity. Increasing their number would allow them to carry out more enquiries, holding ministers to account and scrutinising legislation at the same time. The changes would also create new positions for MPs – as chairs of sub-committees or rapporteurs – and therefore establish an alternative, and much-needed, career path for MPs in parliament. Not least, it would weaken some of the whips' power, as they control the only current career option – promotion to ministerial office.

But the committees should not purely be scrutinising – they should also be legislative. They should have rights to put forward legislation and to have the services of the parliamentary draughtsmen or outside help in drawing it up. This would mean that the same body is responsible for scrutinising the relevant government departments in a policy area, doing the solid committee stage work in parliamentary bills on that area, and also putting forward legislation in areas where they are expert. The Select Committee on the Armed Forces Bill has some power to do this every five years. Others should also be given more power to initiate legislation.

These changes should also look for new ways of engaging the public in the political process. One of the biggest weaknesses of the way parliament examines legislation is that the public has no chance to comment. As every MP testifies, it is through the lives of their constituents that they understand how legislation operates at ground level. This experience needs to be brought into Westminster. Deliberative mechanisms could be used as part of the legislative and accountability process, directly informing parliamentary debates and committee inquiries. The internet now allows for new forms of engagement, including virtual policy consultations. For example, the Womenspeak project organised by the Hansard Society allowed 200 women who had experience of domestic violence to give evidence to the All Party Domestic Violence Group, on a secure, moderated website.[30] More than 9 in 10 of the women felt that the process was worthwhile and said they would be willing to participate in something similar again. A similar number felt they had also learned something from each other's contributions.

A major innovation which would give citizens more power over government is the use of citizen's initiatives. Where citizens collect enough signatures – for example 1 per cent of the electorate – they could propose new laws to be considered by parliament and public inquiries. In particular, this would prevent very unpopular pieces of legislation from being passed – the poll tax is an example. Citizen's initiatives work well in a number of places including Switzerland and Uruguay. This constitutional device can create a real democratic buzz. For example, the streets of Montevideo are full of activists of all persuasions collecting signatures against particular laws, and as a result people talk about these issues in cafés and at home.

A reformed House of Lords could play an increasingly important role. A reformed chamber could experiment with innovations for engaging the public. But it first needs to be elected. It is an absurdity that hereditary peers still have a place in our democratic institutions. And it is to the detriment of this government that one hundred years after Labour first pledged to do away with them, they remain in place. Experience in other democracies across the world suggests that it is possible to have two elected chambers without creating problems of competing legitimacy, and suggestions have been made about ways to elect the second chamber on a different basis, perhaps with regional representation. The Commons should remain the primary chamber, but the proper role of a second chamber in checking and improving the quality of legislation and scrutiny requires that it is able to challenge government, and that legitimacy can only come through election.

Other UK constitutional reform

We need to look again at the electoral system. The strength of the first-past-the-post system is that it usually produces single party majorities in Parliament, making it easy to form governments after an election. But it is a highly undemocratic system. It is unrepresentative: in 2005, Labour formed its majority of 67 (55 per cent of the seats) with just 35 per cent of the vote. The first-past-the-post system forces parties to focus on the concerns of around 30,000 voters in key marginal seats, while millions in safe seats are relatively neglected in what should be a vital and exciting contest for their votes.

Proportional representation would be a fairer system for national elections. Different kinds of PR are being used in many different elections in the United Kingdom including in Northern Ireland, Scotland's local elections and in London. We should take a democratic route to electoral reform through a deliberative process involving citizens, followed by a referendum. We could learn from the process used in British Columbia in Canada, where 160 randomly selected citizens deliberated for a year on electoral reform. The British Columbia government agreed to hold a referendum on their findings and be bound by them.

It is not good for democracy that the government of the day has the power to fire the starting gun on an election campaign at a moment of its choosing. The Commons should have fixed, four-year terms, coinciding with those for the Scottish Parliament and the Welsh National Assembly (and, if in being, the Northern Ireland Assembly).

The devolved experience, particularly in Wales, shows how the executive can operate in a more transparent manner. The Scottish Parliament has shown how to develop 'e-democracy' using e-consultations and online petitions, and we should follow its lead in the creation of a Public Petitions Office in the House of Commons, so that the public can put issues directly on the parliamentary agenda.

There needs to be greater disclosure at all levels of the political system of lobbying.[31] Over 15,000 lobbyists operate in Brussels, and the numbers in the UK are not known. Most represent business interests. Political representatives should record formal and informal meetings with lobbyists, and make these available on a searchable database. There should also be long 'cooling off' periods before government officials can start working for lobby groups.

The relationship between the judiciary and the executive is increasingly strained, and constitutional uncertainty exists over their respective roles; crucially, parliament is largely absent from this relationship. And the shift away from a political to a quasi-legal constitution is set to continue with a number of important developments: reform to the role of the Lord Chief Justice (and Lord Chancellor); establishment of the Judicial Appointments Commission and Supreme Court; and the removal of the Law Lords from Parliament. Combined with an increase in judicial review and decisions under the Human Rights Act, this means we will see more, not less, judicial activism. Such developments are likely to increase the tension between the executive and judiciary and further heighten the confusion and uncertainty over their respective roles.

If parliamentary sovereignty means anything then parliament needs to play a stronger role in this. There is a need for greater parliamentary oversight of judges. With the creation of the Supreme Court, the Law Lords are now leaving the House of Lords, and this argues the need to find more ways for judges to communicate with parliament. For example they could appear more regularly before select committees to discuss their role, as is currently happening with the Constitutional Affairs Committee. They could also hold an annual session with a specially constituted parliamentary committee, following the model of the Monetary Policy Committee, whose members are scrutinised by the Treasury select committee.

We need a new Civil Service Act which amends the doctrine of ministerial responsibility so that ministers are accountable for policy, and strategy and civil servants become externally accountable for operational matters.[32] This would enhance the power that parliament has to hold civil servants – a major part of the executive – to account.

UK constitutional reform has sometimes been seen as a panacea. It is essential for democracy, but it is not enough. It needs to be accompanied by many other measures, including strengthening civil society, improving participatory democracy, democratising the economy and workplace and changing democratic culture. And since we now live in a globalised world, democracy also needs to be global. The next chapter addresses this major issue.

5 European and global governance

The issue of international and global governance is crucial in the changing world we live in. Democracy is no longer an issue that can be tackled solely at the level of the nation state. Many major issues we face today, such as climate change, international crime, migration and epidemics, are not things that can be solved nationally. There need to be layers of democratic governance right the way from local to global, including new institutions where they are currently not in existence. Non-state and international governmental actors need to be held to far greater account. We need to engage in a strategy that encourages much greater working between nation states, and also involves intergovernmental organisations (such as the International Labour Organisation) to strengthen global governance and democracy.

Promoting democracy in the wider world

Democracy and human development go together.[33] Democracy is part of human development: political freedom is a human right. Democracy also protects people from catastrophes – for example Amartya Sen has shown that democracies have far greater incentives to avert famines than undemocratic states. And democracy can create a virtuous circle of human development: people can use their democratic freedoms to push for social and economic policies that meet their needs.

As we have argued, democracy is not just about elections, although these are important. Democracy needs a culture and a set of institutions, including independent media, a vibrant civil society, separation of powers, well-functioning political parties, human rights, civil liberties and civilian control of military forces. The form these take will be different depending upon local circumstances, but they need to be embedded for democracy to take root. Aid budgets should focus on promoting these democratic conditions, which are a fundamental basis for long-term human development. As recent events have reaffirmed, democracy cannot simply be imposed on a country from the outside.

In terms of promoting democracy more widely, the European Initiative on Democracy and Human Rights has been bureaucratic and inflexible. It could be replaced by a 'European endowment for democracy' modelled partly on the

National Endowment for Democracy in the US, but run in a more democratic and transparent way.[34]

Europe

The European Union badly needs renewal. It was established to build peace and prosperity on our continent – to draw a line under the long, bloody struggle between France and Germany, to sweep away trade restrictions that divided the Member States from each other, to counter the perceived threat from the Soviet bloc, and to pool national sovereignty in key areas to strengthen Europe's role in world affairs. But today, the first three objectives have either been achieved or rendered irrelevant, and the fourth has foundered on a lack of unity and legitimacy. The recent constitutional collapse served to highlight the EU's failures in identifying a new vision, more relevant to the twenty-first century. Meanwhile the Union has undergone successive enlargements, multiplying the number of member states by a factor of four since the early 1970s. Europe has come to seem remote and technocratic – a matter of unbelievably complex wheeler-dealing between different groups of politicians, bureaucrats and lobbyists, with little input from its citizens. Almost certainly, these developments explain the withdrawal of public interest and support for the EU, declining participation rates in European elections, and the 'no' votes in 2005 in the French and Dutch referendums on the proposed constitution.

We must address the crisis of legitimacy by working to weave together a Europe of free federal states based on principles of subsidiarity and collective action. Subsidiarity means power begins at the bottom and is delegated upward. So it could provide an effective basis for a cosmopolitan democracy, joining nation-states and citizens across borders.

As a first step, a 'democracy kernel', saved from proposals for the European Constitution, should be taken forward now.[35] It would consist of three modest reforms. First, there would be a requirement for the European Council to meet publicly, forcing transparency upon member states. It is not acceptable that the EU is able to make key political decisions in secret. Secondly, there would be a right for a third or more national parliaments to 'call in' proposals and send them back for revision. Thirdly, and most importantly, there would be a European citizens' initiative, allowing a right of proposal if citizens raise a million signatures. This would allow citizens to have a sense of direct connection with and power over the EU.

Alongside this, Europe must work harder to protect civil liberties as it takes a more active role in Justice and Home Affairs (JHA). There needs to be more scrutiny of JHA legislation by the European Parliament. EU governments should also agree on standards for the rights (for example, to legal aid, translation, etc) of defendants who face trial in EU countries other than their own.[36]

These proposals should be presented as a proof of intent to respond to the referendum 'No's, tackle the legitimacy crisis and move decisively forward. Only then can a new mission, centring on the twin causes of cosmopolitan democracy and global survival, be adopted, and the tools to deliver this put together. *A New Political Economy* considers how we might become more embedded within a 'social Europe'. Beyond this, even in the United Kingdom more than half of us support more pooling of sovereignty at European level in the areas of foreign and defence policies.[37] In the wake of the Iraq disaster, this might not be a bad place to start. There also needs to be a redoubling of effort and ingenuity on the environment, beyond Kyoto – where Europe could lead the way.

Global governance

The debate about global governance is at a nascent stage and nobody has the answer although there are some developing ideas.[38] Some more specific ideas on global governance are put forward by the other two Compass *Programme for Renewal* books. Here we focus primarily on the overall approach and mechanisms. We need to create better representation and regulatory capacity at the global and regional levels as a complement to national state power and more local power. How can we do this?

Creating treaties between countries or new institutions can be too slow to deal with the pressing nature of the issues that we face. One proposal for dealing with this is to create global issues networks in the shorter term.[39] These would comprise representatives of a range of stakeholders, including governments, NGOs, business, etc, who have expertise around a particular issue (e.g. migration). They would develop policy recommendations for specific problems, and seek to put formal and informal pressure on all of the relevant different actors to enact the solutions. Whilst this cannot be seen as a substitute for the creation of new treaties and institutions, it is a worthwhile step in speeding up such processes.

We should also encourage parliaments of nation states at a regional level (e.g. Latin America), which can create regulation at the supra-national level. As argued in *A New Political Economy*, countries need more power over setting their own economic policies, rather than being forced to follow the neo-liberal prescriptions of the IMF and World Bank. Such institutions also need to be made more open to greater poor country involvement, and public representation and scrutiny.

For example, in the World Bank, the same team designs, appraises, and presents projects to the Board, and then holds the country accountable for the success of the project. The countries should be permitted to design their own projects, hiring their own experts. Such a reform would free up projects from Bank ideology, making them far more relevant to local conditions, and providing an opportunity to use local wisdom. This move will end the practice whereby the Bank appraises and approves its own projects. Similarly, there needs to be action to make the Bank partly accountable for the failure of projects that it has approved and financed. Currently, the only feedback on unsuccessful projects takes place through the reports of the powerless Operations Evaluation Department, and its reports have little impact. It would be better to have an independent arbitration board, consisting of legal, financial, and development experts, to investigate the reasons for failed projects, or harm caused by Bank-financed projects.

At the same time as making these quasi-governmental institutions more accountable, we need to make sure that other international players, including NGOs and other agencies (e.g. large donors such as the Gates Foundation), are also made accountable. These private organisations wield incredible influence and operate in the public domain, but with few mechanisms of accountability.

There is a need to create new international institutions and mechanisms where they are currently weak or lack enforcement power. At the moment, the effective machinery of international governance is heavily biased towards market-oriented agencies such as the WTO. This needs to be offset with better institutions to address environmental and social issues – *The Good Society* suggests the creation of a World Environment Organisation as an example of this. International institutions need to be made more democratic; at present they tend to make decisions in remote and undemocratic ways and are subject to strong corporate lobbying. We can also experiment with referendums that cut across nations, including at regional and global levels – although it is acknowledged that referendums need to be used with care, as they are no substitute for programmatic politics.

In the long term the world will need to strengthen the capability of global deliberation to deal with global issues. This could come from reforming the UN General Assembly or by creating complementary institutions. The recent Princeton Project on National Security advocated the creation of a new 'Concert of Democracies' as a way to strengthen co-operation amongst liberal democracies. Any global forum will, of course, be difficult to sustain, but without bodies capable of debating between nations, agreeing action and holding participants to account, our global capability to tackle issues such as climate change, or to create law enforcement and peace-keeping capacity at a global level, remains dangerously weak. As the major problems we face become global in nature, democracy needs to become global to deal with them. We need to experiment with new kinds of institutions, regulations and networks internationally, to create a new kind of global democracy for this century. The UK is well placed to begin this debate through our links with the US, the Commonwealth and through Europe.

6 Civil liberties and human rights

Our basic liberties and human rights are a fundamental part of democracy. They safeguard us against arbitrary abuses of power, enable us to participate in political decisions, and require public justifications for policies and practices which interfere with our rights and freedoms. True democracy is not simply about converting the majority will into political action but also about standing up for the rights of the excluded and of minorities.

The Human Rights Act was a major step forward for democracy, providing an explicit recognition of a limited range of fundamental rights and freedoms in UK law. It is a sophisticated piece of legislation, designed to balance rights. But over the past few years the government's commitment to human rights has been waning. When government has found human rights to be administratively inconvenient, such as in the areas of immigration and asylum or counter-terrorism, it has dismissed the courts' use of the Act as undemocratic, or threatened to amend the terms of the Act. And the media has misrepresented the Act as a charter for criminals and terrorists, focusing on a small number of high-profile cases. The thousands of cases, within and outside of the courts, in which the Human Rights Act has helped the most vulnerable have largely gone unreported. This is all in a context where our civil liberties are being eroded and police powers are being strengthened in a variety of ways that are detrimental to our freedom.

The West has stood in judgement for many years over the human rights record of other countries when they have argued that terrorism or conflict prevented them from abiding by internationally agreed standards. But we now hear our government making the same excuses. Of course we need to defend ourselves against new threats. But Tony Blair's argument that 'traditional civil liberty arguments are not so much wrong as, just made for another age' is mistaken. Nobody questions the need for new approaches and regulations to meet new threats. But we should not let these erode the liberal foundations upon which our society is built. After all it is our respect for the dignity and worth of all people – the very principles which underlie human rights – which separates civilised societies from the terrorists who seek to destroy them. The many failures of intelligence that have occurred in recent years – such as in the case of Jean

Charles de Menezes, the man shot dead at Stockwell tube mistaken for a terrorist, or in the incident in Forest Gate where 250 police stormed an innocent Muslim household and shot a man – show that we cannot give carte blanche to our security forces. There must be adequate controls to protect the innocent. Civil liberties need guarding most in times of threat, as these are when rights are eroded.

Terrorism is not an 'enemy' against whom a 'war' can be waged: it is a global social phenomenon. As the Club of Madrid has argued, terrorism comprises 'criminal acts to be handled through existing systems of law enforcement and with full respect for human rights and the rule of law', and a key antidote to terrorism is 'the systematic promotion of cultural and religious dialogue through local encounters, round tables and international exchange programmes.'[40]

We need to safeguard and strengthen our civil liberties and human rights. What are the means by which we should do this? A reinvigorated parliament, as described in the chapter on national constitutional reform, could help to prevent the erosion of civil liberties. But there are also other opportunities.

Shorter term opportunities

The starting point must be to build an awareness of rights. A number of important steps have been taken towards the promotion of human rights principles in Britain. A new Equality and Human Rights Commission is to be established, to champion equality and human rights. In addition, human rights education has become part of citizenship education in schools. We should build on this work. One of the greatest attributes of human rights principles is their accessibility; unlike most other laws you don't need a law degree to understand them. Despite this, many people continue to see human rights as the reserve of the terrorist or criminal, and many urban myths abound. Public agencies have an important role in creating a 'human rights' culture; their managers and staff need to be part of a wider education process, making sure their actions don't inadvertently breach rights and helping the public to understand their rights; and not using the Human Rights Act as a 'knee-jerk excuse' when things go wrong.

As part of preserving our civil liberties we should not proceed with UK identity cards.[41] They will not protect us from terrorism – they would not have stopped 9/11 or 7/7. They will not cut crime – they are no deterrent in countries that already have ID cards. In fact they might create a new host of crimes using fake ID cards. Nor will they stop benefit fraud. More than 90 per cent of benefit fraud is based on people using their own names but continuing to work cash in hand whilst on benefits, or on convincing a doctor that they are too ill to work. The cards will cost each person at least £93, and it seems likely that costs will rise, as has been the case with many large government IT projects.

We also need to renew our commitment to the right not to be tortured. A case can be made for most human rights to be restricted where this is necessary to meet a pressing social need, such as public safety. Torture, however, can never be justified. The absolute prohibition on torture requires states to do more than merely ensure that torture does not happen within their territory. It also requires us not to deport people to places where there is a real risk that they will be tortured; to ensure that evidence obtained by torture is not used in British courts; and to make sure that we are not complicit in torture anywhere else in the world. The danger of undermining these wider aspects of the prohibition on torture is demonstrated by the practice of 'extraordinary rendition' – the transference of suspects to states that practise torture, with the aim of gaining intelligence. There are widespread allegations that western democratic states have participated in this practice, which is, in effect, the 'contracting out' of torture. There is growing evidence that UK airports and airspace have been used by CIA planes involved in it. If we really believe that torture is wrong we cannot keep our hands clean by letting other countries do the dirty work. This approach needs to be embedded within a broader process of promoting human rights and civil liberties in other countries, as argued in chapter four.

Future opportunities and challenges

There are three major areas where we need an open public debate, to explore how human rights might develop in the future.

One area of exploration would be about moving beyond the public/private divide. The requirement to act compatibly with human rights currently only applies to 'public authorities'. The Act has not provided legal redress for individual victims of rights violations by powerful private bodies; for example, the right to freedom of speech and association has been denied to people demonstrating in a privately-run shopping centre, and individuals in a privately-run residential care home have been denied the right to respect for their home. When they are operating in the public realm, private bodies should be required to comply with human rights standards.

We might also promote a public debate about whether or not to improve upon the rights protected by the Human Rights Act. For example, the Act does not guarantee the right to free legal assistance to those who cannot afford to pay for it. The right to a fair trial could be extended to guarantee the right to legal aid. Nor does the Human Rights Act confer any specific rights in the context of immigration and asylum – should this be addressed? Our current Act does not create any stand-alone right to equal treatment, it only requires that enjoyment of the other rights in the Convention are secured without discrimination. The Canadian Charter, on the other hand, creates a right to equal treatment, and expressly permits positive discrimination.

A third area of debate would be around whether or not our society supports economic and social rights. The Universal Declaration of Human Rights promised protection of both civil and political rights, and economic, social and cultural rights. Civil and political rights are the kinds of rights with which we are most familiar – they include important safeguards like the right to life, the right against torture and the right to a fair trial. Economic and social rights, which include things like the right to work, the right to housing and the right to education, are less familiar. But such economic and social rights are preconditions of the enjoyment of many civil and political rights.

Realising economic and social rights often requires significant financial investment and the weighing of competing considerations. But we might follow the approach of the Indian Constitution, which recognises civil and political rights as legally enforceable but also recognises economic and social rights as 'directive principles'. The Constitution states that economic and social rights 'shall not be enforced by any court' but that they 'are nevertheless fundamental in the governance of the country and it shall be the duty of the State to apply these principles in making laws.' The Indian Supreme Court has drawn upon these principles to identify within the 'right to life' the right to basic accommodation and the right to free education, on the basis that these are preconditions of a full and meaningful life.

Human rights cannot be introduced or enforced without a social consensus. But human rights are a cornerstone of democracy. They protect the individual from arbitrary interference. The UK has a good human rights framework, but it needs to be explained and defended, in order to win public support – so that we have the basis for an informed public debate about whether to extend it further.

7 The media in democracy

The media are inescapably part of the public realm, and a crucial part of the democratic framework of our society. Diversity of the media, access to news and information from the widest range of sources, and accurate and honest reporting, are considered to be vital for guaranteeing pluralism of opinion, adequate political representation, and a citizen's participation in a democratic society. Media pluralism also should serve democracy by facilitating understanding between conflicting groups or interests; promoting cultural variety and exchange; and facilitating social and cultural change, particularly when it provides access for weak or marginal social groups.

The world of the media is undergoing real change at present, in ways that cannot be fully predicted. Old boundaries are breaking down. The rise of 'new media' means that there is the potential for democratisation as media becomes more interactive. Now anybody can comment on pieces in the *Guardian* website, and indeed create their own blog sites. The public realm used to be physically limited, but now a virtual public realm creates an infinite space. The question is, however, what values will dominate it. The changing nature of the media world means that policy-makers need to analyse the shifts that are occurring and think through how to achieve their aims. New questions are thrown up – how do we maintain a public sphere on the web for communities and interest groups to congregate, communicate and campaign? But as well as new questions, the old power realities are still important – whilst the web provides more spaces for democracy, it is also space that is being colonised by existing interests.

The market can contribute to media pluralism but it cannot secure or guarantee it. Communication rights cannot be contingent upon private ownership and control of media. The market also fails to generate adequate incentives to produce and maintain high quality content, or to distribute enough diverse content to meet consumer and citizen needs and preferences. Even where markets are not restricted by concentration, producer power or advertisers' influence, they do not fully or adequately respond to people's preferences or needs, and tend to offer a much smaller range from which to select than people might wish for. Preferences for less advertising and commercialism, or for exposure to new cultural forms, or for education and other so called 'merit goods', are very difficult – if not impossible – to express in the commercial marketplace.

Rebuilding the relationship between media and politics

The media – especially the print media – can take a highly cynical approach to politics, and this contributes greatly to disengagement from representative politics. Opportunities are repeatedly taken to suggest that politicians are corrupt or liars, and invariably the focus is on policy failure rather than policy success. There is a culture of contempt for politics, rather than one of well-researched and critical challenge. Politicians have had to respond to the power of the media through changing how they communicate, with more 'spin', but this in turn has lowered trust.

One proposal to rebuild the relationship between media and politics is to set up a Standing Commission on the Media.[42] It would celebrate good journalism and highlight good practice, commission research and provide for better public scrutiny of media outlets. It could be combined with an Open Commission on Accuracy in the Media, where citizens could take a participative role in promoting accuracy of the media by pointing out inaccurate stories online.[43] These bodies in combination could help hold the media to greater public account and help to rebuild the relationship between media and politics, which in turn could reduce some of the dissatisfaction felt about representative politics.

Tackling media ownership

Across western economies, there has been a shift towards policies favouring media concentration, convergence and integration. This has occurred in the context of a broader shift, from regulation for pluralism towards neoliberal regulation favouring market mechanisms. In the UK, New Labour has tempered market liberalism with a social market defence of public service broadcasting and retention of some media ownership rules. However, the Communications Act 2003 entrenched Labour's massive shift towards market liberalisation and preference for market solutions over regulatory interventions. It removed restrictions on foreign ownership of TV, further weakened the newspaper merger rules, and permitted increasing concentration and cross-ownership across radio and television broadcasting. The Communications Act actively encourages the growth of large media groups. For instance, the Act enabled the merger of Carlton and Granada to create a single ITV, owning franchises across the UK. This has led to subsequent closing of regional production centres, job cuts, and the cutting back of public service obligations. Labour also established the communications regulator Ofcom, an unelected organisation which is charged with increasing competition in mass communications and which operates with a 'bias against regulation', and in favour of commercial market expansion and 'self regulation'.

Globally, a handful of powerful media groups now control an expanding media and leisure market, spanning film, television, book publishing, music, online media, theme parks, sport, the print media and even the theatre. Deregulation has boosted the commercial power of global corporations, but it also gives them political power. They are currently demanding even greater relaxation of rules on media ownership, spending enormous sums on political donations while lobbying key politicians. For instance, the notorious provision enabling Rupert Murdoch to acquire Channel Five, and secure a toehold in terrestrial television, was inserted into the Communications Bill at the last moment, after News Corporation had directly lobbied Number Ten to relax further cross-ownership rules.

Public concern about corporate and political dominance over media and information services is greater than ever. Confidence among readers, viewers, listeners and users of information is low, and there is an increasing perception that journalism is failing to carry out its watchdog role in society, because of the vested interests that drive the media business. Not surprisingly, politicians are worried, too. The media concentration process has paralysed policy-makers and it is time to stimulate fresh debate and prepare concrete actions to confront the challenge of corporate power in mass media.

The public's need to be properly informed means that information services must be regulated beyond the market framework of ratings, profits and commercial objectives. It is also vital that people have access to the widest range of ideas and imagery and space to create and share communications. The problems of media ownership are not restricted to possible limitations on the supply of news and information, but include commercialisation and the erosion of cultural diversity. With increasing integration, there arises actual or potential conflict between editorial integrity and the commercial or corporate interests of firms.

The rise of new media is a potential force for democratisation. It means that citizens who are online have a far wider variety of media outlets through the internet, and in fact can create their own. Examples such as the 'online anti-establishment TV channel' 18 Doughty Street, and the independent online magazine Open Democracy, show what can be done. But the reality is that there are anti-competitive tendencies in the media world which need careful regulation. Google's acquisition of YouTube and News Corporation's acquisition of MySpace show how the new media is both concentrating and also being bought up by old media. These trends need careful watching.

Our aim must be a diverse and plural ownership structure, with a strong public service sector at its heart, accompanied by regulation that ensures long-term investment in high quality content and services. Communications regulation needs to be based on the recognition that the media contribute to pluralism, diversity and quality of information and require a separate regulatory structure from that which governs other parts of the national and global economy. In the medium term this will require changes at national, European and WTO levels to limit the concentration of media ownership through merger, anti-trust and cross-ownership legislation. It would also imply divesting existing media properties where there are unacceptable levels of concentration. At present the debate about media ownership is muted but it needs to move up the agenda.

Public Service Broadcasting and Media

A public service system means that all of the audience have the right to equal access to the whole broadcast output, and that the values of information and education are given equal priority with those of entertainment. Public service broadcasting means producing programmes designed to cover the widest possible range of output. It means educational and arts programmes, news and current affairs. It also means comedy, soaps, drama serials, sport, films, quiz shows and light entertainment.

Public service media provision must be extended in the twenty-first century. There is scope to revitalise pubic service media through greater access and involvement, by extending public service media deep into local communities. However, the BBC and public service media are under serious and sustained attack. It is therefore vital that the institutional and operational strength of the BBC is protected and that wider public service requirements are restored.

Nearly 50 per cent of all viewing and listening in the UK is to the BBC – an environment that carries no commercials at all. It also leaves the UK uniquely placed in terms of world media. Maintaining the strength of the BBC should be a key goal. The BBC needs to be developed as a public service broadcaster, funded by the licence fee. But it should not be the sole public service broadcaster in a commercial media system. The major providers of broadcasting and media services should be required to adhere to key public service values. Ofcom itself has outlined a variety of ways to intervene to develop public service broadcasting, including a levy on new entrants into the UK TV market, tax incentives and direct government grants. Some kind of plurality in key public service broadcasting areas such as news and current affairs would help to maintain quality. This might be through direct funding for other suppliers such as Channel 4 and ITV. It is unlikely that plurality will be sustained without some direct policy intervention.

The licence fee remains a better way of funding the BBC than advertising – though the universal nature of TV consumption suggests it would ideally be financed, more progressively, from general taxation, with ring-fencing to protect it from erosion over time or political leverage by government. 'Top slicing' the licence fee to fund 'public service' programme production by commercial companies would undermine the BBC and remove an incentive from commercial broadcasters to make programmes of quality out of their own income.

The BBC should continue to provide, free at the point of use, services across the whole range of broadcasting, including news, current affairs, original drama, original comedy, radio, music, light entertainment and information services. The BBC should retain its production base and build on it, especially in the nations and regions. It should not sell off its facilities nor privatise any of its departments.

Communications regulation needs to be democratised. In a democracy, decisions about how to organise the media ought to be arrived at following informed debate with widespread public participation. However, as one US media critic puts it:

> once a nation 'deregulates' much of its media to private interests, it is very difficult to maintain public involvement in the policy making process. Private interests are able to use their cultural, economic, and political power to prevent open evaluation of whether they are the proper stewards of the nation's media. Once this 'deregulation' process is near completion, it is very difficult to reverse the process, as extremely powerful interests block the democratic path.[44]

In the UK, broadcasting matters could be devolved to national and regional communication councils. These might include representatives of the national parliaments and assemblies, and people appointed by nominating bodies. The nominating bodies could be organisations that represent people in their workplace and local communities, and they could select people for the communication councils through a process of internal election. They in turn would nominate candidates for election on to the BBC Trust and Ofcom boards. Ofcom could be re-established as a democratically representative body. Its primary job could be the promotion of the public interest in mass communications by stimulating public service values and practices across the media. It could introduce requirements on companies that have a significant share of the audio-visual market to provide public service programming.

Tackling how the media approach politics, changing media ownership rules and protecting public service broadcasting are at the heart of a democratic approach to the media. These changes would help preserve our democracy and revitalise our politics.

8 The role of civil society

C ivil society (or as it is increasingly being known, the 'third sector') is different from the state and the market – it includes voluntary and community organisations, charities, social enterprises, faith groups, co-operatives and mutuals. It is a major change agent that has traditionally been underestimated, although there is recent political interest in it. It is often not included in discussions of representative democracy, but there is more to democracy than representation – there is also association.

The third sector is often the starting point for people's democratic engagement. It has a crucial role in holding other agents (such as government and the private sector) accountable. And a great deal of policy innovation happens through the voluntary and community sector and social enterprises. Civil society plays a crucial role in society as a campaigner and voice, and it is also one significant arena for building social capital and well-being through collective action or just meeting other people. In other words civil society is not just about marginalised communities – it is a way of achieving a whole range of aims.

But civil society is not always benign. It contains reactionary forces as well as progressive ones – such as racists, religious fundamentalists or plain old business lobbies. The truth is that 'civil society' is a diverse sphere. Sections of it can be as bureaucratic as the next state institution. Other sections, like some big NGOs, can sometimes resemble multinational corporations in their unaccountability and global scope. Sometimes 'civil society', littered with experts and professionals, can seem as remote and alienating from everyday life as mainstream political parties. There is, therefore, a need to combine strong civil society with strong democratic structures – each needs the other to be effective

Civil society should not be used as an excuse for the state to step back from the essential duties it performs. We need the state to guarantee fairness and minimum standards. We cannot rely on charity and mutual aid alone to create the good society, although they are crucial components. So we need to think about how to strengthen civil society alongside an active state.

Civil society and democracy

The transfer of power from Whitehall to local councils and then on to communities – or 'double devolution' as it is known – is very welcome, but it assumes that the devolution of power and responsibility must always be from the top to the bottom. It assumes there is a mass market of citizens just waiting there, demanding to be given this responsibility. But democracy is not a market. People have to be genuinely empowered to make them believe democracy can work for them. At the moment they do not.

To place the agenda of citizens, not consumers, at the heart of the reform of national and local government and public services, individuals and communities must be given the skills and the support to take control of their public services or local democracy. In order to devolve power we must first ensure citizens have the skills to feel confident about their ability to influence their local MP or a school governing board. How can this be done? We need to recognise that voluntary and community organisations, not political parties or elections, are the starting point for most people's pathway to broader civic engagement. We can support organisations that bring voice to communities. We need to engage civil society to provide better, more responsive services and to ensure citizens have that voice and the confidence to use it. For example, we might add on to healthcare contracts money to help communities share their experiences of the service or their area.

With good intentions, the government has proposed numerous policy initiatives (particularly at a local level) to draw on the potential of civil society in enhancing democracy and engagement (e.g. New Deal for Communities; regeneration schemes that are characterised as 'partnerships'; Ken Livingstone's community policing initiative). Unfortunately, they have not been very successful in genuinely engaging 'the community'. 'Engagement' is very resource intensive, and any policy proposal that looks at strengthening the grassroots dimension of civil society needs to reflect that in its process; otherwise it will just be tokenistic. But throwing money at the problem will not fix it either. We need to identify genuine models of engagement and look at why they work and how their methods can be made of use elsewhere.

Central government policies cannot easily strengthen civil society – it cannot be strengthened from the top. But what government can do is create conditions that would give rise to a strong civil society. This includes devolving decision-making power, including economic decisions. The state could invite civil society institutions into power-sharing experiments, and include lay people in them. It can support social enterprise through improving access to finance, running markets more explicitly for public benefit and improving leadership and governance in the sector. National and local government need to offer training to support engaged and active citizens. And they should consider increased funding for the 'voice' function of third sector organisations, so that marginalised groups are better represented.

We should consider introducing a certificated national service. People of all ages would get the chance to volunteer to serve the country by performing one or more national service 'units' of at least six weeks, with a variety of bodies, including charities, sports and the arts. By serving at least a six week unit, a volunteer could acquire a certificate worth points, which could be used towards acquiring a modular educational qualification, paying off a student loan or accelerating the rehabilitation period for offenders. Such a scheme could help to engage young people, enhance social inclusion, promote contact between communities and generations and prevent re-offending. Volunteering also provides very strong impacts on well-being and social capital.[45]

At present much funding (including the Lottery, Futurebuilders and Change Up) is moving away from supporting wider civil society organisations to focus on government priorities. The role of non service-providers is being neglected, but often the work that they do is crucial and unique. A government interested in optimising the resources available to civil society would recognise trades unions, universities, voluntary and community-based organisations as having their own legitimacy and accountability outside the state, and their own reasons for action and knowledge about what might work. They should be treated as a resource, and as valuable and knowledgeable partners in their own right. In particular their campaigning role means that they should not get too close to the state, thereby becoming absorbed or overly influenced by its priorities.

Third sector regulation can be a real burden.[46] Good regulation is essential to maintain the trust of the sector and to protect users, beneficiaries and society. But much regulation is target driven rather than focused on needs, and many organisations are subject to multiple regulation (e.g. from the Charity Commission and Companies House). Third sector organisations should be more involved in the development of regulation, and regulators need to take a more joined up approach.

Civil society organisations need, however, to become much more accountable. There can be conflicts of interests in their multiple roles, especially as they increasingly move into service delivery and commissioning. At minimum, organisations in the sector should disclose their lobbying work so that there is transparency about political processes. Third sector organisations need to have good representation from the people they claim to stand for, and be more open to scrutiny and involvement from stakeholders; otherwise they will be a block to democracy rather than fulfilling their potential to be one of the major engines of it.

9 Workplace democracy and trade unions

We cannot be fully fledged citizens if we spend much of our day at work being robots. Democratic principles cannot stop outside of the workplace. Workplace democracy can mean different things in different contexts. What is appropriate in the private sector will be different from what might work in the public sector. Large multinational companies will be different to small and medium sized businesses. For some the only meaningful workplace democracy is the kind of workers' control found in small-scale co-operatives, for others it can mean the vaguest kind of consultation arrangement.

Neither of these will be meaningful to the bulk of the workforce, but employees do want a say when they go to work. Surveys regularly show that the lack of a voice at work is a consistent complaint of UK workers. Only around two in five workers have strong influence over their working hours or the organisation of their work, and fewer than half have influence over access to training.[47] The same research suggests that those workers with the lowest levels of health and well-being are also those least likely to have voice in their workplaces. The other *Programme for Renewal* books consider different aspects of how to spread workplace democracy. In particular *A New Political Economy* argues for reform of company law to make sure that companies take greater account of all stakeholders including their employees and *The Good Society* argues for more employee owned businesses, even if they are unlikely to employ more than a small minority of the workforce.

They may not call it workplace democracy, but what workers want is the ability to shape the decisions that affect them at work. There is abundant evidence that more democratic forms of business and workplace organisation can make good economic sense as well as creating new opportunities for people to flourish in their working lives.[48] Economic incentives at work have some importance, and employees need to feel that they are fairly rewarded, but high morale and staff motivation flow from a much wider range of workplace attributes, such as autonomy, responsibility, high-trust relationships, access to training and development, good quality management and work-life balance. Workers who have a bigger stake in the future of their enterprise and a greater role in determining its future directions and their own working environment will be more committed to their jobs, more cooperative with colleagues, more productive on the job, and more creative problem-solvers and innovators.[49]

For example at Semco in Brazil, teams of employees interview the candidates vying to become their boss. Instead of hiring the one that will give them the easiest ride, they have learned to pick the one that will make the best manager, improving the team spirit and performance of the group as a whole. At Toyota all employees can stop the production line to put forward an idea about improving the product. These workplaces do not have the mythical view that all knowledge lies with the chief executive, but use a far more decentralised model to enable all members of staff to contribute. Giving employees a voice in the organisation should not, however, be seen in just economic instrumentalist terms. Workplace democracy is important as it contributes to the mental and physical well-being of employees, enabling them to lead autonomous lives.

Enterprises with a stronger sense of responsibility to their workforce are more likely to compete through investment and innovation rather than by cost-cutting and short-term labour-shedding. There is a potential for convergence here between the claims of the cooperative tradition (with examples such as the Mondragon co-operative in Spain, which is the seventh largest corporation in Spain), the trade union movement, and progressive management thinking. Without denying the important differences and real dilemmas here, this is the space in which we need to develop a new debate about the future of work and business organisation.[50] Yet UK business organisations appear to be wedded to an old-fashioned view that starts and ends with 'the manager's right to manage'. All public policy interventions are dismissed as red tape, and debate about the poor quality of work organisation and the quality of UK managers is taboo. Government's understandable desire to maintain support from the business community should not prevent them from playing a 'critical friend' role. Of course there is no single model to impose, and all organisations whether public or private have wider accountabilities than simply their staff, but this should act as a spur to creative thinking and experimentation, rather than as an excuse to shut down debate.

In particular, the EU directive on Information and Consultation is to be implemented by 2008, and gives employees the right to be informed and consulted on a regular basis about issues in the organisation they work for. Proper implementation of this by employers – and a more enthusiastic take-up by unions – would help build better and more democratic workplaces.

The role of the unions

One of the most important roles in shaping workplace democracy will come from trade unions.[51] Britain's unions make a key contribution to civil society. With over

7.5 million members, and more than 200,000 activists voluntarily undertaking representative duties in workplaces, they form one of the pillars of our democracy. They provide a vital voice for people at work and act as a key countervailing force to the imbalance of power built into the employment relationship. They are an important part of the public realm and at their best act as academies of citizenship. Even though European style social-partnership is extremely under-developed in the UK, the TUC gives people at work a real voice in Westminster and Whitehall, as can be seen in the recent debate on pensions.

Yet union membership has been in decline. It peaked in 1979-80, fell sharply through the Conservative years, and has remained largely constant at 29 per cent of the employed workforce since Labour came to power in 1997.

Most membership trends flow from changes in the composition of the workforce. The decline under the Conservatives had most to do with restructuring and the decline of manufacturing. The stability since 1997 largely comes from the growth in public sector employment, which roughly balances out a continued decline in the private sector, although this account neglects some positive trends in the private sector, such as growth in retail – largely driven by concentration in the sector – and the media. Declining union membership is a feature of other similar countries, and the UK's recent steady state compares favourably with falls in countries such as Germany.

This should be no cause for complacency. Trends in the world of work are running against union membership. The growth in the public sector will not continue, and the decline of larger long-established (and unionised) employers in traditional parts of the private sector is inexorable, whatever the overall state of the economy. Unions have yet to have much success in breaking into the new service economy. To perform their function in democratising workplaces, unions must come to terms with new challenges, new attitudes and changes in the labour market.

Britain's labour market has been relatively successful in recent years, with record levels of employment and low levels of unemployment. The UK has high levels of employment among women, and, closely connected to this, high levels of part-time working. More jobs require skills, and a growing proportion of the workforce are graduates. The workforce is increasingly multi-cultural, and parts of the economy now depend on short-term economic migrants, mainly from the new EU member states.

There is evidence to suggest that we are in an 'hourglass' labour market. This theory suggests that we are seeing a decline in middle-range jobs, such as skilled jobs in manufacturing, due to the pressures of globalisation, but a growth both in quality knowledge-based jobs at the top end of the labour market, and in poor-quality service jobs (ones that cannot be relocated) at the bottom end of the labour market. It is too early to say whether this is a clear trend, but it may very well be that, while the negative impacts of globalisation are easy to see when closures and off-shoring hit the headlines, the growth of new types of job is less visible. It is too early to see whether these two trends will balance out.

But what is clear is that there is a division between the majority of the workforce who generally tell researchers that they enjoy their jobs, even if they have specific complaints about some aspects, and a substantial minority who face poor treatment, low pay, lack of autonomy and even denial of their legal rights. The media exposure of the rank exploitation of some migrant workers has brought part of this dark underbelly of working life in the UK into public view, but the position of many of the UK's vulnerable workers remains hidden.

Unions therefore face a difficult dual challenge. The workers most in need of union representation are among the hardest to organise. They tend to work in casualised and insecure employment, and face employers extremely resistant to unionisation. While there are some inspiring union success stories – such as the TGWU's work with cleaners in London – organising efforts are difficult and expensive. It will take a combination of measures to make a real impact in this sector: union action; new legal protections – especially for agency workers; the right to engage in secondary action to support industrial action by other workers; and proper enforcement of new and existing rights.

Among the rest of the workforce there is less obvious discontent, and there has been a rise of jobs and whole sectors that lack any tradition of unionisation. Unions have found it extremely hard to make inroads, and density in the private sector now runs at less than 20 per cent.

Surveys still suggest that employees want a voice at work, but while they are not hostile to unions many do not see them as relevant or appropriate in their own workplace. Yet there are enough examples of successful private sector unionisation to show that it can succeed. Usdaw's growth in Tesco and Amicus's partnership arrangements in Legal and General show that unions can grow and build good relationships with responsible employers. The GMB's necessarily more aggressive campaign against Asda has made this a lonely beacon of unionisation in the Walmart empire.

While there are many good examples of innovation in the trade union movement, it is also clear that unions have not always kept up with the realities of today's workforce and labour market. It is therefore time for a debate about modernising trade unionism, and examining all aspects of their work.

This is not a call for weak unions that are too close to employers, but a recognition that the modern world of work is extremely diverse. When faced with rank exploitation, autocratic management and employer hostility it is entirely appropriate for unions to use tough tactics and industrial action. In workplaces with the most vulnerable workers, where unions find it hard to build the strength to use the traditional tools of trade unionism, community campaigning, consumer concern and legal action may be more appropriate. In other workplaces partnership working with progressive employers may be the best way to represent and improve the lot of members.

Unions need to examine how they use their limited resources. In the past unions needed to put significant resources into national negotiations, but industrial relations are now more decentralised and union structures must reflect this. All modern membership organisations need to put considerable resources into marketing and recruitment – or organising, as unions call it. But while there has been a welcome growth in organising efforts, there is still some way to go. It is also important that the appeal that unions make is rooted in the problems and attitudes of today's more femininised and multicultural workforce, rather than harking back to outdated images of the macho trade unionism of the past. And on the ground organisation needs to be supplemented with better international alliances, as Amicus is exploring. Since capital is transnational unions must also organise globally. Unions need to become both more local and more global.

The public face of unions in the workplace – the union reps – do not always get the support and assistance they deserve. In some cases barely half the stewards regularly receive union support materials like handbooks, employment law guides, bargaining briefs or health and safety advice. Training can be inaccessible – it is often based on the view that employers will give time off and will pay for the course. There needs to be more accessible training, including distance-learning provision. Many stewards now feel isolated, being the only union representative at their workplace. By 1998 some 25 per cent of workplaces where unions were recognised had no union steward. This means no one to represent existing union members and no one to enrol new recruits as existing members retire, change employers or lose their jobs.

While unions are rightly proud of their democratic structures, there is a debate to be had about how best to involve and engage members today. The world of branch meetings and complex structures may well be past its sell-by date. They can, at their worst, be expensive to run, and end up serving only a self-perpetuating small group of activists. This is not to suggest that there is a new model that will fit all unions. Just as different strategies are needed in different workplaces, different unions need to find different ways of engaging members that work in their sectors. Big general unions require a different approach to small specialist unions. But as the Musician's Union have shown, it is not impossible for a union to completely overhaul their democratic structures to cut out bureaucracy and involve members. New technology makes it easy for unions not only to communicate with their members but also listen to them.

By working together unions and employers have the potential to deliver dramatic improvements, boosting productivity and profitability and enhancing living standards and future prospects. Allowing workers more power over the running of their organisation can unleash their creativity and improve productivity. Mutual commitments to co-operation and a problem-solving approach to employment relations can free up management time, promote effective team working and improve dignity at work. Similarly, shared commitments to customers, colleagues and the company can reduce labour turnover, cut absenteeism and produce a better work-family life balance. Common commitments to find more flexible ways of working that suit both employer and employee can cut customer order lead times, boost motivation and morale, and enhance job satisfaction.

Shared commitments to training and personal development, which make continuous improvement a reality, can ease the take-up of new technology, promote quality and precision, and enhance employability. And mutual commitments to accident prevention and risk avoidance can streamline production, boost reliability and make workplaces safer.

The agenda of unions should broaden to consider issues of 'good work' as described in *A New Political Economy*. There should be more focus on fulfilling and creative work, better work-life balance and more training and career development services. Unions also need to broaden their agenda to take into account environmental issues, given this is a major issue for workers everywhere. The TUC has taken a lead on issues around 'greening the workplace', and there are other initiatives such as the Trade Union Sustainable Development Advisory Committee. More unions need to embrace these, and to create wider alliances with groups that are pushing for sustainable energy, green buildings and better public transport.

Workplace democracy can be a real win-win. An active approach by employers to give employees more control over their working lives and a revived trade union sector would not just be intrinsically worthwhile – it would also lead to more productive workplaces and to happier and more fulfilled employees. This is a crucial step to put the UK economy on the 'high road' to prosperity as described in *A New Political Economy*.

10 Realising the public realm

As our lives become increasingly dominated by capitalist relationships and commodification, the spaces in the public realm become a key place in which we learn to share, to work and act together, to protect the weak and to act as guardians of our social wealth for future generations. Public parks, public libraries, schools, concert halls, theatres and swimming pools are some of the few social spaces where people from all social classes can come together – where they are not segmented and targeted by age or income.

It is because private sector values can be inimical to values of equality and fairness, and corrosive of social cohesion, that the public realm must have within it the power to control and constrain the private sector. It is because the drives of self-interest, accumulation of profit, and competition, are at odds with social values of sharing, mutuality and collaboration that we need social spaces in which non-market values prevail. It is within the public realm that, for example, our children learn to constrain and contextualise the values learned in capitalism – greed and instant gratification. Collective endeavour is not simply a second-best to private consumption. Through taking part in a march, a charity run, a vigil, a community function, a trades union, a school concert – we satisfy a basic human need for expression as part of a group, a collective. Not only is there such a thing as society, but it is a rich and diverse place, full of encounters with the unexpected and opportunities to learn from others.

History teaches us that 'public goods' are not fixed economic categories, but have been won by the political campaigns of the past two centuries. Extended by nineteenth-century reformers to include water, gas, electricity, telephones and public parks, and again in the second half of the twentieth century to include health, clean air, river quality, national parks, comprehensive education, universities, theatres and concert halls, public goods are once again under attack – as gated communities reduce a sense of collective safety, and as playing fields, libraries, post-offices and allotments disappear. There have been a few, brave, attempts to extend public goods into new areas – for example, the right to roam – but, by and large, New Labour has been content to accept the neo-liberal view that public goods are what's left over when the market has provided everything else.

Public space and the environment

Public spaces and public buildings are central to the public realm and should be protected. We need a moratorium on the sale of all school playing fields and public recreational land for private use. School playing fields, allotments and school buildings should be seen not as belonging to the individual service but to the local community as a whole. Finding multiple uses for buildings and seeing them as community resources rather than as simply 'office accommodation' will help to make better use of them. PFI schemes offer short-term gain but saddle the public sector with long-term costs and constraints. A shift to a more sustainable capital programme will involve rethinking costs and benefits over a fifty to one hundred year time scale, rather than the lifetime of a government.

Many different and competing social and political goals come together at the point at which public services are delivered, and finding ways to balance between those different goals – achieving as many as possible – is only possible on the ground. For example, schools should be seen not simply as 'education factories' – buildings used to get children to pass exams – but the hub of a wide range of educational, cultural, sports and training activities, for kids, parents and the surrounding community. Linking schools into their surroundings, accessed in the evenings by adults undertaking training and at weekends by communities – for dance, football, gardening or reading clubs – would change thinking about both education policy and the use of public buildings and begin to bridge the growing divide between generations.

The Good Society considers the responsibility of the individual for the future of the planet, and *A New Political Economy* discusses the role of tax, regulation and the private sector. The public sector has a key role too. Local authorities, public agencies and their communities should be expected to take a lead on environmental measures. This is already happening. Central government has pledged that it will become carbon neutral by 2012. Manchester has begun a campaign to get local people to respond to the needs of the planet, and aims to reduce the city's greenhouse gas emissions by 20 per cent by 2010. Every city and town should develop its own target for emissions, water conservation and other environmental indicators, and have the power to persuade the public and private companies to play their role. Dialogue about ways to achieve these goals should form part of Local Communities Strategies. Where growth is planned, this should be expected to have a neutral environmental footprint – and radical thinking about how this is to be achieved should engage both the immediate locality and wider region in discussion that moves beyond 'nimbyism' to a realistic appraisal of the challenges to be overcome.

Public services and the public realm

Public services are a key part of the public realm (whether or not they are delivered by the state) and underpin the values of the good society. Social justice, equality of opportunity, work-life balance, dignity and respect cannot be achieved without high quality public services accessible to all. Exhortation and voluntary effort, while commendable, never achieve much without the involvement of the state. The quality of the lives of most citizens has most often been dramatically improved through government action – even though this has often been a result of social pressure and organisation. Clean air, clean water, universal health care, pensions and public transport have ultimately all been achieved through action involving the state.

The House of Commons Committee of Public Accounts outline a number of criteria which provide a picture of what underpins good public services.[52] They must understand the needs of users and design services in that light, and consult users regularly. Public services must have good and flexible delivery mechanisms, and monitor service performance to learn lessons and innovate. They need to employ and motivate capable staff, provide redress when things go wrong and do what they say they will. Some public services are like this, but many are not.

Equality must be at the heart of public services, regardless of who they are delivered by. Of course different kinds of service delivery will often be necessary to achieve equality and not everyone wants exactly the same outcome. But research shows that the poor pay more for their services and get less.[53] For example, paying household bills by direct debit can save individuals over £70 a year, but 8 per cent of households do not have a bank account. Poor people often have less access to services because of limited transport or disability. Ethnic minorities, disabled people and older people face additional barriers to using public services, and their needs are not always well understood.

The odds continue to be stacked against the disadvantaged. In the top 200 state schools poorer pupils are massively under-represented, with only 3 per cent of pupils qualifying for free school meals, compared with a national average of 14 per cent. In this way public services work to the detriment of the life chances of disadvantaged people when in fact we need to promote them. *The Good Society* advocates the Fabian Society's notion of a 'life chances litmus test' to evaluate all policies for their impacts on life chances. If we design public services in ways that meet the complex needs of the worst off, they are more likely to work for all users. Public service reform for improved life chances needs to be set within a broader programme to increase equality and reduce poverty and exclusion, as described in the other two volumes of the Compass *Programme for Renewal*.

Public service renewal

There can be no going back to the 1970s. State provision, without exposure to proper accountability and challenge, has a tendency over time to 'decay'; to bureaucratise, be prone to supplier capture and to centralise. Public services need built-in counter pressures to make them responsive, innovative and accountable. We need a democratic state, ensuring professionalism, constant improvement and healthy competition, with a plurality of providers, including the private and voluntary sectors. Accountability needs to be close-up and personal. We need high quality, responsive services, and redress if the experience is a bad one. No one is arguing about these things.

Many of the changes that have taken place in public services over the past twenty years have been positive. Public services have been exposed to the discipline of responsiveness, while private companies have begun to learn how to work in partnership. However, our vision of public services remains constrained. The alternatives are seen as either what Charles Leadbeater has called the 'McKinsey state' – driving public services through a vast bureaucratic public corporation, using crude sticks and carrots – or, alternatively, the resort to the equally crude mechanisms of the profit motive and the market.

The current approach to public services treats them as 'products' to be delivered through vast, capital-intensive projects, that use technology to distance users further and further away from the service. Professionals and staff feel more and more alienated from a targets culture that treats them simply as cogs in a machine – robots for producing service 'results'. Most of the problems that society faces, such as an ageing population, the environment or chronic disease, are outside existing service boundaries.

We have seen the introduction of markets across a range of public services. The government has introduced the three Cs of an efficiency agenda – contestability, choice and commercialisation. But these are a largely untested route to improvement, and the results that we do have are mixed.[54] In local government we have a relatively successful mixed economy of provision with, for example, some leisure and waste services having improved. But this approach does not always work so well in highly complex services, such as education and health. Despite massive investment in academy schools, research from Edinburgh University shows that the number of pupils getting five GCSE A*-C grades, including English and maths, has increased only by 0.2 per cent (equivalent to three pupils each) across the first 11 academies. And academies are also less likely to be connected into a wide array of local provision and services, unlike the radical experiments with community schools with shared sports facilities, libraries and meeting spaces. Similarly, hospital cleaning, the service that has longest been open to market forces, is now cheap but fails to meet the required standard.

There are not enough cleaners, we have a casualised workforce and there are high levels of infection in hospitals. The speed of the introduction of markets into the health service has led the Audit Commission to warn that some hospitals may go bankrupt in performing the high-cost operations that nobody else wants to do. The Kings Fund has noted of all the changes to the NHS that 'it is clear that the results of their interaction may be at best unpredictable and at worst perverse'.

Market mechanisms, unconstrained, have tendencies equivalent to state provision to decay. They can turn complex social outcomes into 'products', poorly serving users with complex needs and failing to integrate with other services. They can waste money through poor project management, negotiate deals that serve the public ill and extract super-profits from public taxpayers. They can be phenomenally complex. The PPP contracts for the London Underground are 28,000 pages long. This means the transaction costs are very high, as the lawyers need to be called in whenever somebody wants to do something different. Governance structures are opaque: contracts tend to be kept secret due to commercial confidentiality, despite the strong public interest component to them.

The introduction of private sector providers can create innovation but this is not always the case when there is no real diversity of supply and we end up with monopolistic providers, as is the danger in health at the moment. The transfer of risk out of the public sector can be a good thing, and this has been the justification of PFI contracts which raise finance in a more expensive way than public finance. But often there is little risk transferred. Services provided under PFI and PPP schemes are insulated from market pressures and guarantee a steady stream of income for years. Exit from contracts can be costly to the public sector – for example Bedfordshire county council had to pay £7.8m to HBS when it sacked it for poor performance on a £250m contract.

The folly of dogmatic policy is best exemplified by an example in Australia of the use of PPPs. The £300m cross Sydney toll tunnel was built as a PPP, and was supposed to relieve traffic. But the private sector got its predictions wrong and most motorists did not use it. This led to the local city authorities closing off alternative routes in an attempt to make motorists pay for the tunnel! We have plenty of instances showing these kinds of tensions in the UK. For example, until 2010 many private hospitals have had thousands of operations pre-purchased, but given rules on patient choice it is unclear how they can be guaranteed the flow of patients if people do not choose to go there.

Because the drive to make profit adds costs, waste resources and raises prices, we must allow that often the cheapest, most efficient form of production is through public investment and publicly run provision. It is no accident that the American healthcare system is the most expensive in the world, with spending at

16 per cent of GDP – almost twice the OECD average.

The role of the private, public and third sectors

While all three sectors have a role to play, the overall balance of provision should be managed and shaped by democratically accountable organisations to ensure that they achieve public goals; private providers must be subject to regulation and control if they want to work in the public realm. Markets that rely on public funding must operate in the public good. Markets in the public realm are not like private markets, since public money and government conditions distort outcomes, and providers are highly protected from market risk. Government has a role in designing the conditions for entrants to the market, planning supply and skill-mix; in the inspection and regulation of quality and the prevention of abuse; the public assurance of public values such as equity and justice; and in holding the private sector accountable for its actions.

This means clarifying the expectations we have of private sector organisations in the public realm – including a fair sharing of risk, sensible provisions for when private organisations fail, or wish to exit, and protection of public assets. Local authorities should have a direct role in managing local markets for public services, supported by regional market expertise, and national policy that sets a protective legal framework to deal with market failure and regulation.

We need to design 'quality markets' where regulation specifies a high quality of service. The public transport market in London is a good example of a quality market, where there has been specification of which routes should be provided, what a fair price is, and of acceptable waiting times.[55] All providers have either had to meet this challenge or exit the market. By contrast, many bus routes outside of London where there has been less regulation have fallen prey to unfair competition, where big private providers have used their financial muscle to drive out competitors through predatory pricing. So designing quality markets with a diversity of provision is crucial when engaging in public service reform. Otherwise we will create monopoly provision by a small number of private sector providers. The government seems to have learned from its experience in buses and is considering reregulating bus routes outside of London: this is welcome but the experience casts light on a far wider range of markets.

The third sector can play a number of valuable roles in the reform of public services.[56] Government needs to pay more attention to the role civil society organisations can play in helping to identify service gaps and designing new ways to meet needs, rather than simply expecting them to deliver current services more cheaply. Government must begin by fully involving the third sector in decision-making about what the needs are and what is commissioned – this should lead to more joined up commissioning. When it comes to delivery of public services, we must ensure that money to be spent on engaging service users is included in the contracts. There should also be greater investment in the sector to create the capacity to meet the challenges of public service delivery and to innovate. Government must ensure that community organisations taking a role in public service delivery are properly supported, and are not simply exploited as cheap providers.

It is about time we also recognised the new professionalism, management expertise and success of public services. This is most evident at the local level, where local authorities are becoming increasingly efficient through a self-confident combination of out-sourced and in-house services. It is nationally run public services that seem, in contrast, to be bureaucratic, slow and incompetent. But the myth that the public sector is bureaucratic in comparison to the private sector is simply not true. Research shows that the private sector has more so-called 'bureaucratic' jobs than the public sector, and the public sector has a much leaner management structure than the private sector, even when taking into account differences in workplace size.[57] Research shows that the public sector is as innovative as the private sector (if not more so), but the diffusion of innovation is faster and deeper in the private sector.[58] We need to experiment with new mechanisms to spread innovation and make institutions more responsive.

A different approach

The top-down centralised behemoth could be replaced with a looser, more organic network of services that fit the needs of the people who use them. Instead of crude assumptions about central control ensuring 'delivery', we need to pay more attention to how complex systems work. Systems theorists point to radical approaches to improvement – used by Toyota and others – that rely on accurate feedback and the relationship between front-line workers and users to drive improvement.[59] They show how targets distort outcomes. For example, the target that all people should be able to see a GP within 48 hours led to many surgeries not taking bookings beyond a 48-hour period. Patients wait in ambulances outside A&E to comply with targets that measure the time between entering the hospital and seeing a doctor. Crude output measures tend to encourage 'cheating', and can crowd out the complex local decisions that can optimise value. This implies the need for a bonfire of targets and the need to involve all stakeholders – including employees and users – in decision-making.

We need to develop systems that are centred on the needs of individual citizens and promote innovation and initiative among professionals, rather than rely on vast centrally controlled programmes. Such systems would use technology to underpin delivery on a human scale. They would harness the expertise and skill of front-line staff and the behaviour and motivation of service users, and capitalise on the powerful benefits of good relationships and reciprocity between the providers and users of public services. We could look for inspiration at projects such as PledgeBank.com (see p27), or Neighbourhood Fix-it, a project to improve communication between people in neighbourhoods and their local authority about environmental improvements.[60]

The appropriate form of governance for this era is what has been described as 'citizen-centred' or 'networked'.[61] Its focus is not the maximisation of choice for individual consumers, but the creation of value for the public. Individuals are not considered as atomised but as diverse; their 'preferences' are not taken as given but their needs as complex and volatile, and prone to risk. Public provision would not be primarily through markets and contracts with large private sector companies, but through networks and partnerships, embracing the full range of non-governmental organisations.

At its heart is a process of iterative dialogue, engaging policy-makers with practitioners and users, as well as civic leaders. The diverse, complex and dynamic nature of contemporary social challenges means they tend to be perceived differently by different stakeholders, and they are not subject to linear solutions delivered within one organisational silo. Monitoring and evaluation is thus inevitably qualitative as well as quantitative. Contracts between 'purchasers' and 'providers' can never capture such richness and uncertainty, and targets can never provide more than very rough proxies for success or failure.

In the Nordic model, the state plays a key enabling role, but critical to success is a dense and wide network of associations and institutions. Policy is not decided at the centre and then simply 'delivered' on the ground. In this approach, policy itself is elaborated through a process of dialogue that not only avoids sub-optimal outcomes but also engages a range of actors in the collective purpose of taking ownership of the policy and so making it happen.

Involving citizens

Services should be closely tailored to individual needs. Public and voluntary sector providers should be expected to engage in dialogue with users to co-design the exact package of provision to meet their needs. Good primary care achieves this, as do direct payments to social care users – or tailored provision for children excluded from school. At the local level, we have the potential to use technology, pooled budgets, integrated services and partnerships, a plurality of providers – to tailor services to individual or neighbourhood needs, planned in consultation with users or groups of users. We can learn from examples across the world. For example the Chicago police department has held monthly community meetings in over 200 of its beats since 1995 to discuss community safety strategies with residents and to design these together.[62] Around 5000 citizens attend these each month, particularly poorer citizens who are more affected by crime.

Many of the things we want as citizens – places for children to go, safe streets, cohesive, safe communities, less waste, less congestion – cannot be achieved by a smart government delivery machine. To achieve these things we have resources at our disposal not limited to those we can buy in the market place. These include collective action, moral pressure, tolerance, compassion, charitable efforts and reciprocal support. But these resources cannot be commanded by the centre. Nor can they be bought in the marketplace. They require people to change their behaviour. The only possible route is for the state to engage in dialogue with citizens, individually and collectively, about how best the investment of state resources can support the resources of the public.

Citizens need to be treated not as passive consumers but as 'activist-providers' playing a role in achieving social outcomes alongside government, and 'co-producing' services that use public resources to maximum effect. This is what cutting edge experiments in public services are examining; there is much to be learned from collaborative methods such as those used by Alcoholics Anonymous, and from peer-based communities such as the Grameen micro-finance bank in Bangladesh.[63] Nobody has all of the answers on how to do this; but it requires sustained innovation and distributed power, which are manifestly absent from most public services at present, regardless of who is delivering them.

Social capital

Human beings thrive on their relationships. Social capital is the glue that holds communities together. Workplaces with strong networks and relationships generally outperform those without. And, nationally, social capital seems to contribute to both human well-being and economic performance.[64] Not all social capital is good – criminal networks or old school ties are not progressive. But social capital is a key ingredient in making things work well.

When putting forward progressive policies, we should consider how to strengthen social capital or at the very least how not to destroy it inadvertently. In particular there is a need to invest in social capital that 'bridges' between communities, or links citizens to people in power. When we consider inequality, we must look at unequal social networks as well as unequal resources, as they are both crucial. For example, most people find out about their next job through somebody they know. Public service reform must be careful not to inadvertently destroy relationships which have built up over many years, and which constitute the informal knowledge of the organisation.

Finding resources for the public realm

Emphasis on local solutions and on networks that directly engage service users will make the best use of scarce resources. The proposals made earlier in this book on devolution, and on shrinking government radically at the centre and the regions, could release resources to the front line. While some areas of public provision face rising demand – such as health – it may be possible to reduce the cost of good services through a more human, flexible approach, using local ingenuity and creativity, by developing care and treatment pathways that support people in their own choices, and by combining the resources available at local level more effectively.

The real financial limitations of the public sector can only be tackled through steepening the tax gradient – essential in any event to redress the inequalities which pervade the UK. But reductions to spending controlled by central government could devolve billions of pounds to providers on the ground. Continual pressure for improvement, and opportunities for service providers to think radically about re-designing services with and around the user, can continue to improve our public services and the public realm.

Afterword

There are no magic answers, no miraculous methods to overcome the problems we face, just the familiar ones: honest search for understanding, education, organization, action that raises the cost of state violence for its perpetrators or that lays the basis for institutional change – and the kind of commitment that will persist despite the temptations of disillusionment, despite many failures and only limited successes, inspired by the hope of a brighter future.

Noam Chomsky

Did you, too, O friend, suppose democracy was only for elections, for politics, and for a party name? I say democracy is only of use there that it may pass on and come to its flower and fruit in manners, in the highest forms of interaction between [people], and their beliefs – in religion, literature, colleges and schools – democracy in all public and private life ...

Walt Whitman

Notes

1. Ian Shapiro, *The State of Democratic Theory*, Princeton University Press 2003.

2. Roger Levett et al, *A Better Choice of Choice*, Fabian Society 2003.

3. Lord Hailsham, 'Elective Dictatorship', The Richard Dimbleby Lecture, *The Listener*, 21.10.76.

4. BMA/MORI poll, *Trust in doctors*, 2005, available online at ww.bma.org.uk/ap.nsf/Content/MORI05.

5. Power Commission, *Power to the People*, Power Inquiry 2006.

6. Geoff Mulgan and Fran Bury (eds), *Double Devolution*, Smith Institute 2006.

7. Privacy International, *Privacy and Human Rights Report*, Privacy International 2006.

8. Work Foundation's Work and Well Being survey, quoted in David Coats, *Speaking Up!*, Work Foundation 2005.

9. Emily Keaney and Ben Rogers, *A Citizen's Duty*, ippr 2006.

10. For example see Ron Johnston et al, *Sleepwalking to segregation?*, CMPO, Bristol Institute of Public Affairs 2006.

11. Tom Bentley, *Everyday Democracy*, demos 2005.

12. Richard Titmuss, *The Gift Relationship*, Allen and Unwin 1970.

13. Geoff Mulgan, 'The remaking of democracy', in Richard Wilson (ed), *Post Party Politics*, Involve 2006.

14. See for example Robin Murray et al, *Open Health*, Design Council 2006.

15. Meg Russell, *Must Politics Disappoint?*, Fabian Society 2005.

16. Stuart White, in 'Markets, Time and Citizenship' (*Renewal*, Vol 12 No 3, 2004), argues for limiting the working week on the basis of time being a necessary condition of citizenship.

17. Graham Smith, *Beyond the Ballot*, Power 2005.

18. Involve, *People and Participation*, Involve 2005.

19. Commission on Poverty, Participation and Power, *Listen Hear*, Policy Press 2000.

20. Neighbourhoods Initiatives Foundation – www.nif.co.uk.

21. John Healey MP et al, *MPs and politics in our time*, MORI and Hansard Society 2005.

22. Stephen Coleman, *Direct Representation*, ippr 2005.

23. Meg Russell, *Must Politics Disappoint?*, Fabian Society 2005, p55.

24. John Healey MP et al, *MPs and politics in our time*, MORI and Hansard Society 2005.

25. See for example Jon Cruddas and John Harris, *Fit for purpose*, Compass 2006, which provides many ideas on how the Labour Party could renew itself.

26. Fiona Mactaggart et al, *Parties for the Public Good*, Young Foundation 2006.

27. Geoff Mulgan and Fran Bury (eds), *Double Devolution*, Smith Institute 2006.

28. Graham Smith, *Beyond the Ballot*, Power 2005.

29. See Graham Smith, *Beyond the Ballot,* Power 2005; Archon Fung and Erik Olin Wright, 'Deepening Democracy: Innovations in empowered participatory governance', *Politics & Society*, Vol 29 No 1, 2001.

30. Graham Smith, *Beyond the Ballot*, Power 2005.

31. See for example www.alter-eu.org/./statement.

32. Guy Lodge and Ben Rogers, *Whitehall's Black Box*, ippr 2006.

33. Human Development Report, *Deepening democracy in a fragmented world*, UNDP 2002.

34. Centre for European Reform, *EU 2010: A programme for reform*, CER 2006.

35. Paul Hilder, *Trumpets round the city walls: from divides to democracy in Europe*, Fabian Freethinking paper 2005.

36. Centre for European Reform, *EU 2010: A programme for reform*, CER 2006.

37. Eurobarometer 64, autumn 2005. In the UK, 59% already support more of a common European defence policy, and 50% are for a common foreign policy, while only 34% are against it – and young people are even more positive.

38. The ideas around global governance are most well developed by David Held at the LSE. This section is largely based on ideas contained in chapter 6 of David Held, *Global Covenant*, Polity 2004.

39. Based on ideas by Jean Francois Rischard. See David Held, *Global Covenant*, Polity 2004.

40. See The Madrid Agenda agreed at the International Summit on Democracy, Terrorism and Security, 11.3.05, at http://english.safe-democracy.org/agenda/the-madrid-agenda.html.

41. Liberty, *Fiction and Fact*, 2004 (available online at www.liberty-human-rights.org.uk/privacy/id-cards-fiction-and-fact.shtml).

42. Meg Russell, *Must Politics Disappoint?*, Fabian Society 2005.

43. Geoff Mulgan et al, *Wide Open: open source methods and their future potential*, Demos 2005.

44. Robert McChesney, *Theses on Media Deregulation*. Submitted to Campaign for Press and Broadcasting Freedom, July 2002.

45. Hetan Shah and Nic Marks, *A Well-being Manifesto*, nef 2004.

46. See for example Margaret Bolton, *The Impact of Regulation on the Voluntary Sector,* NCVO 2004.

47. Work Foundation's Work and Well Being survey, quoted in David Coats, *Speaking Up!*, Work Foundation 2005.

48. See, for example, M.J. Conyon and RB Freeman, *Shared modes of compensation and firm performance: UK evidence*, NBER Working Paper W8448, 2001.

49. See for example CIPD, *Understanding the People and Performance Link: Unlocking the Black Box,* CIPD 2003.

50. David Coats, *Speaking Up! Voice, Industrial Democracy and Organisational Performance*, The Work Foundation 2004.

51. For a more detailed analysis, see Kevin Curran, *Organising to Win*, Compass 2006.

52. House of Commons Committee of Public Accounts, *Delivering high quality public services for all*, Sixty-third report of session 2005-06, House of Commons 2006.

53. Georgia Klein et al, *Paying more, getting less*, National Consumer Council 2004.

54. Which?, *Which? Choice: can the government's choice agenda deliver for consumers* 2005, www.which.co.uk/about_us/A/campaigning/consumer_choice/Choice_report_559_54957.jsp.

55. NERA Economic Consulting, *The Decline in Bus Services in English PTE areas*, Passenger Transport Executive Group 2006.

56. Ann Blackmore, *How voluntary and community organisations can help transform public services*, NCVO 2006.

57. Economic and Social Affairs Department, *Bowler Hats and Bureaucrats – myths about the public sector workforce*, TUC 2005.

58. Geoff Mulgan and David Albury, *Innovation in the Public Sector*, Prime Minister's Strategy Unit 2003.

59. Jake Chapman, *Systems Failure*, Demos 2002; John Seddon, *Freedom from Command and Control*, Vanguard Press 2003.

60. See www.pledgebank.com and www.mysociety.org.

61. These terms are from John Benington. See Robin Wilson, 'Two wrong calls: the third term horizon', *Renewal*, Vol 11, No 3, 2003.

62. Graham Smith, *Beyond the Ballot*, Power 2005.

63. Robin Murray et al, *Open Health*, RED – Design Council 2006.

64. David Halpern, *Social Capital*, Polity 2005.

About Compass

Compass is the democratic left pressure group whose goal is both to debate and develop the ideas for a more equal and democratic society, then campaign and organise to help ensure they become reality. We organise regular events and conferences that provide real space to discuss policy, we produce thought-provoking pamphlets, and we encourage debate through online discussions on our website. We campaign, take positions and lead the debate on key issues facing the democratic left. We're developing a coherent and strong voice for those that believe in greater equality and democracy as the means to achieve radical social change.

We are:

- An umbrella grouping of the progressive left whose sum is greater than its parts.

- A strategic political voice – unlike thinktanks and single-issue pressure groups Compass can develop a politically coherent position based on the values of equality and democracy.

- An organising force – Compass recognises that ideas need to be organised for, and will seek to recruit, mobilise and encourage to be active a membership across the UK to work in pursuit of greater equality and democracy.

- A pressure group focused on changing Labour – but Compass recognises that energy and ideas can come from outside the party, not least from the 200,000 who have left since 1997.

- The central belief of Compass is that things will only change when people believe they can and must make a difference themselves. In the words of Gandhi, 'Be the change you wish to see in the world'.

Compass
FREEPOST LON15823
London
E9 5BR
t: 020 7463 0633
e: info@compassonline.org.uk
w: www.compassonline.org.uk

Join today and you can help change the world of tomorrow

Please contribute generously. Compass is funded solely by organisations and individuals that support our aim of greater equality and democracy. We rely heavily on individual members for funding. Minimum joining rates are suggested below. To join, simply complete and return this form to Compass, **FREEPOST LON15823, London, E9 5BR**. Paying by Standing Order or Paypal means we have a regular income to count on, consequently we are offering new members a discount for paying their membership in this way. To join by Paypal you will need to go to the Join Us section of the Compass website at www.compassonline.org.uk/join.asp.

☐ Waged (SO / Paypal) – min £27.50   ☐ Waged (Cheque / PO) – min £32.50

☐ Unwaged (SO / Paypal) – min £12.50   ☐ Unwaged (Cheque / PO) – min £17.50

☐ Organisation (i.e. CLP; think-tank; NGO) – min £42.50

Name

Address

Postcode

Telephone

Email

If you're already a Labour member what is your CLP?

Positions held

Standing order instructions

Please pay immediately by standing order to Compass' account, Lloyds TSB, 32 Oxford Street, London, W1A 2LD (a/c 2227769, sort code 30-98-71) the sum of £10 / £25 / £40 / Other £ (please delete as appropriate) and then annually, unless cancelled by me in writing.

Bank / Building Society

Bank Address

Account Name

Account Number   Sort Code

Signature

☐ I'm not eligible to be a member of the Labour Party (i.e. you're a member of another political party in the UK) and I would like to become an Associate Member of Compass (with no voting rights).

compass

DIRECTION FOR THE DEMOCRATIC LEFT

The Good Society
COMPASS PROGRAMME FOR RENEWAL

MEMBERSHIP OFFER

Join Compass and get the 5 *Programme for Renewal* publications including *The Good Society* edited by Jonathan Rutherford and Hetan Shah

From just £12.50 make a stand today for greater equality, democracy and freedom

Get annual membership from just £12.50 when you join by standing order and receive the five '*Programme for Renewal*' publications. Join using the form on page 90, alternatively you can join online using Paypal at www.compassonline.org.uk/join.asp.

New members joining Compass will over the coming months receive 5 excellent publications

Visit our website and join online at www.compassonline.org.uk

building
democracy

A better voting system may not solve all the problems of our democracy, but without electoral reform we cannot move towards a new and more engaging form of politics.

As a Society member, you will be sent our regular magazine, *The Voter,* and other briefings, and you will be able to play a part in shaping our policies and programmes.

Members joining before the end of June will be sent a free copy of *Britain's experience of electoral systems* with 150 pages of analysis (priced £8), recently published as the Society's response to the Government's delays in publishing its own review. Membership costs only £10 p.a. (£5 for those on low incomes).

For more information on the Society and an application form, visit us online: www.electoral-reform.org.uk

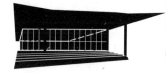

Help build
democracy
Join Us.

☐ Electoral
☐ Reform
☐ Society